In Ran
Running

In Ramallah, Running

Guy Mannes-Abbott

ArtSchool Palestine
منتدى الفنون المعاصرة

SHARJAH ART FOUNDATION

black dog publishing
london uk

Contents

Introduction

Jean Fisher

Introduction

Jean Fisher

> Man said: blessed are the birds in their cages for they, at least, know the limits of their prison. Mourid Barghouti [1]

In Ramallah, Running is a rare project. A set of palpable explorations in and around the hills of Ramallah transformed into a text and then remobilised in dialogue with a variety of artists' responses. It produces the exceptional sense of being drawn into the lived interior of a place known primarily by the external pressures exerted against it. What unfolds in these pages is testimony to a place of deeply etched surfaces, experienced sometimes joyously, sometimes with acute frustration, which speaks across time. It is a place starkly at odds with the abstract, militaristic geometry that seeks its destruction.

As Guy Mannes-Abbott discovers through his exchanges with local people, 'running' is not a common spatial practice among the residents of Ramallah and its hinterlands. Maybe it is a luxury pursuit only the foreign visitor with time on his hands—or afflicted with an excess of curiosity—can afford; or maybe, like Barghouti's birds, suspended in a perpetual present, the residents are now too wearily aware that there is nowhere to run to or from without encountering soul-destroying or life-threatening limits. Nonetheless, it is a truism that to create limits is also to create the conditions for transgressing them, if not overtly then by subterfuge—and both manoeuvres are operative here. If there is something a tad foolhardy in Mannes-Abbott's rising to

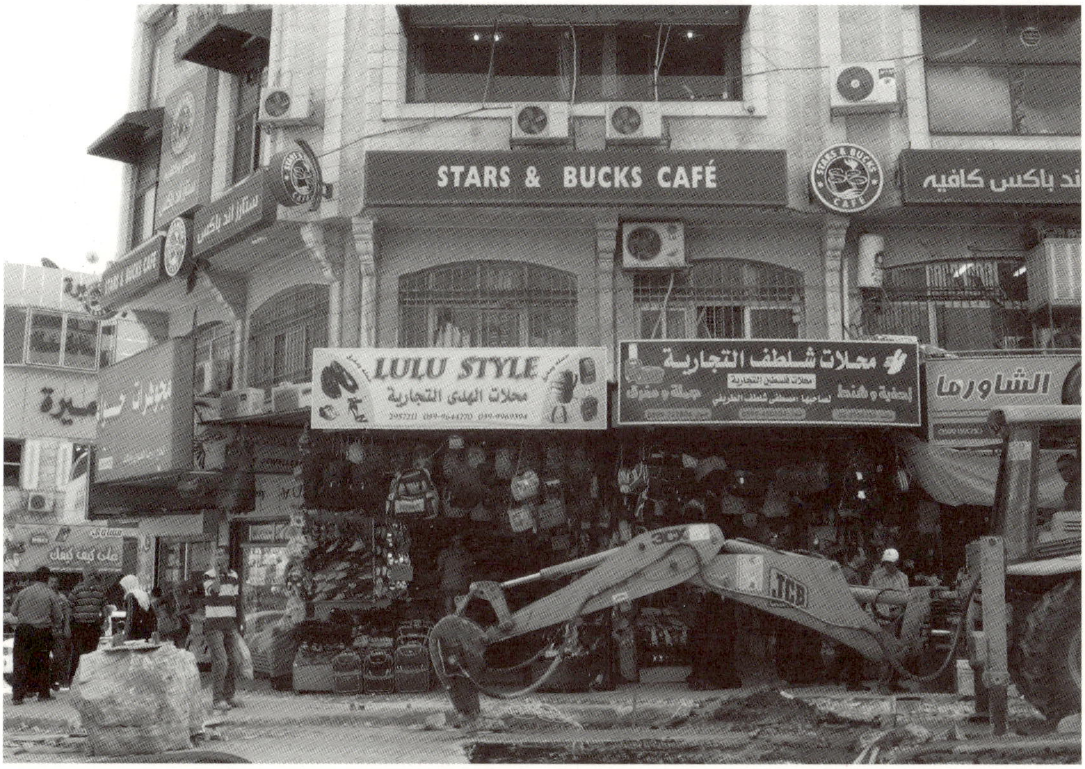

Stars and Bucks,
al-Manara Square.
Photography copyright
Jean Fisher.

Introduction

Jean Fisher

the challenge by testing the limits of these limits, it is also indisputable that his transgressions perform a topographic *détournement* of which the spatial abstractions of cartography bear little trace.[2] If we may indeed call the motor that drives Mannes-Abbott's running "curiosity", it is nonetheless curiosity with a purpose, infused with "what is..." and "what if..." questions that need to be asked even if the answers remain stubbornly elusive. Two immediate questions come to mind: What does running reveal of experienced, lived-in truths, concealed behind the smoke and mirrors of those who claim "Palestine" does not exist? What does Ramallah itself signify? Mannes-Abbott runs to see the lie of the land....

Resonant throughout these pages is an unsettling interface, as concrete as it is volatile, between contestatory notions of space: what Henri Lefebvre called that "perceived space" organically produced by lived experience and the "conceived space"—spectacular, 'abstract'—of cartographers, urban planners, property speculators and colonisers.[3] "Perceived space" is what Mannes-Abbott evokes as "place". "Place is", as he puts it, "worn, freighted, complex. Space is seductive, abstract, dust free." And undermining the assumptions of both is the "third space" of the imagination, which knows no limits.

Ramallah, October 2010: I am as yet unaware that Mannes-Abbott has recently been running along these roads and out towards these austerely beautiful hills. Naïve visitors like myself, virtually parachuted into the centre of Ramallah, may be forgiven for thinking that this city is like any other undergoing a vigorous regeneration programme. Building sites are everywhere refurbishing streets, planting trees, constructing new suburban housing and, notably, high-rises reputedly for corporate commerce and tourism. The visitor has, indeed, to look and listen attentively to penetrate this facade of normality. Little by little the general cedes to the particular: the rutted scars in pavements left by IDF tanks during Israel's periodic 'incursions'; the silence of air space (pace the occasional surveillance drone); little gems of early twentieth century domestic architecture abandoned to nature; the crates in the fruit and vegetable market that reveal them to be Israeli produce, a crude reminder that this produce is largely grown in land stolen from Palestinian farmers. As Adania Shibli so poignantly writes here, truth in this city is to be found in such "trivial and minor details" as the sale of "rotten lettuce for a king's ransom". Perhaps most

Al Bireh vegetable
market with Israeli
packaging/supplies.
Photography copyright
Guy Mannes-Abbott.

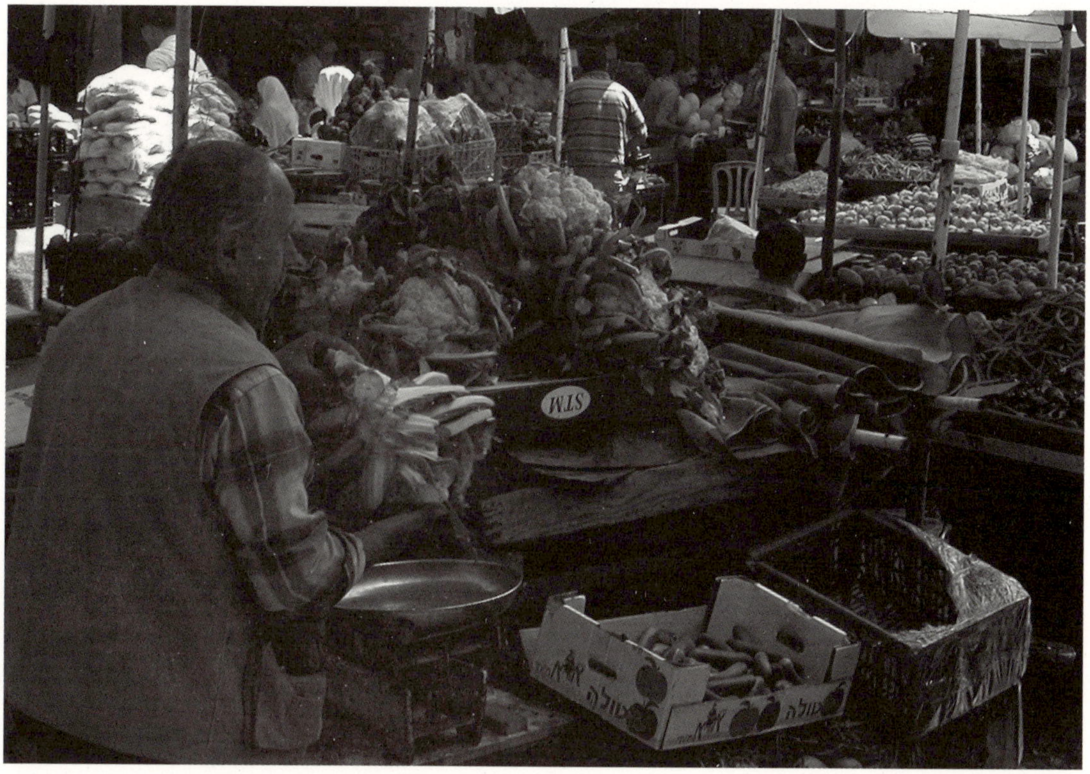

Introduction

Jean Fisher

affecting is the "Stars and Bucks" café in al-Manara Square. If other signs testify to the physical stresses of Occupation, the café is witness to an aspiration to be reunited as equal speakers in a cosmopolitan conversation, a connection cruelly severed some 60 years ago. Here, then, is a little gesture of resistance to enforced isolation from the 'outside' world.

Mannes-Abbott's focus, at first glance, is less on the city itself than its environs. But as Shibli's text curls inwards, into a claustrophobia relieved only by the uncertain horizon of a stand of pine trees seen from a window, so in a complementary, centrifugal move his excursions curve out from the centre. They produce precisely that anamorphic gaze whereby an object is revealed by adopting a de-centred, ob-scene angle of vision.

The author's ob-scene excursions reveal 'other' truths through an embodied, sensuous engagement. His narrative leads us out of the city, up and down the *wadis* and terraces of the Ramallah hills, noting their vistas, remnants of ancient olive groves once lovingly tended by countless generations, native flora and fauna. Here we are given to imagine the taste of Palestinian coffee (strong and spiced with cardamom), or of bread fresh from the *taboon*, there to catch the scent of wild sage, or, more ominously, the stench of rotting garbage. It is perhaps Jananne al-Ani's contribution to these pages that most evokes the underlying regret in this endangered rural landscape. Her photographs present details of murals, weathered and faded, from a tiny school house in the hamlet of Yanun, south-east of Nablus: an image perhaps of a visit to the city, now almost impossible due to Israeli restricted passes and checkpoints; a landscape depicting water flowing through a wadi overseen by the Palestinian sun bird, a small glimpse of vivid greenery revealed through a hole in the wall; another pastoral scene of a bird—perhaps another sunbird, or a thrush—perched in the foreground and overlooking a grazing donkey. These are less idealised images than records of inhabited surfaces fondly known, intimately experienced.

In Mannes-Abbott's narrative the threat to this time-honoured world is laid bare in the same breath that invokes its contours. For elsewhere we trip over live ammunition or tear gas canisters near an illegal settler compound, or hear the crackle of radios and screech of military vehicles in pursuit of spatial 'violators' who have crossed the line of the permissible. Everywhere, with each sortie outwards, we are

BELOW & OPPOSITE
Handmade terraces and qasr strewn wadi linking Surda and Ain Qiniya, marking Ramallah's northern extent. Photography copyright Guy Mannes-Abbott.

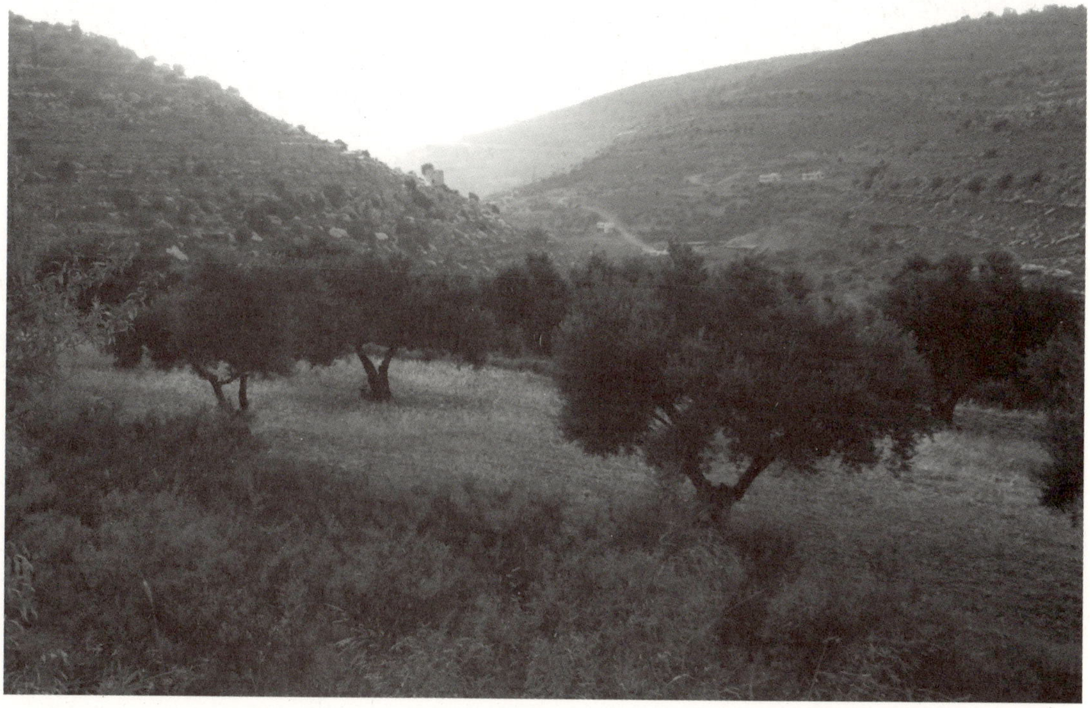

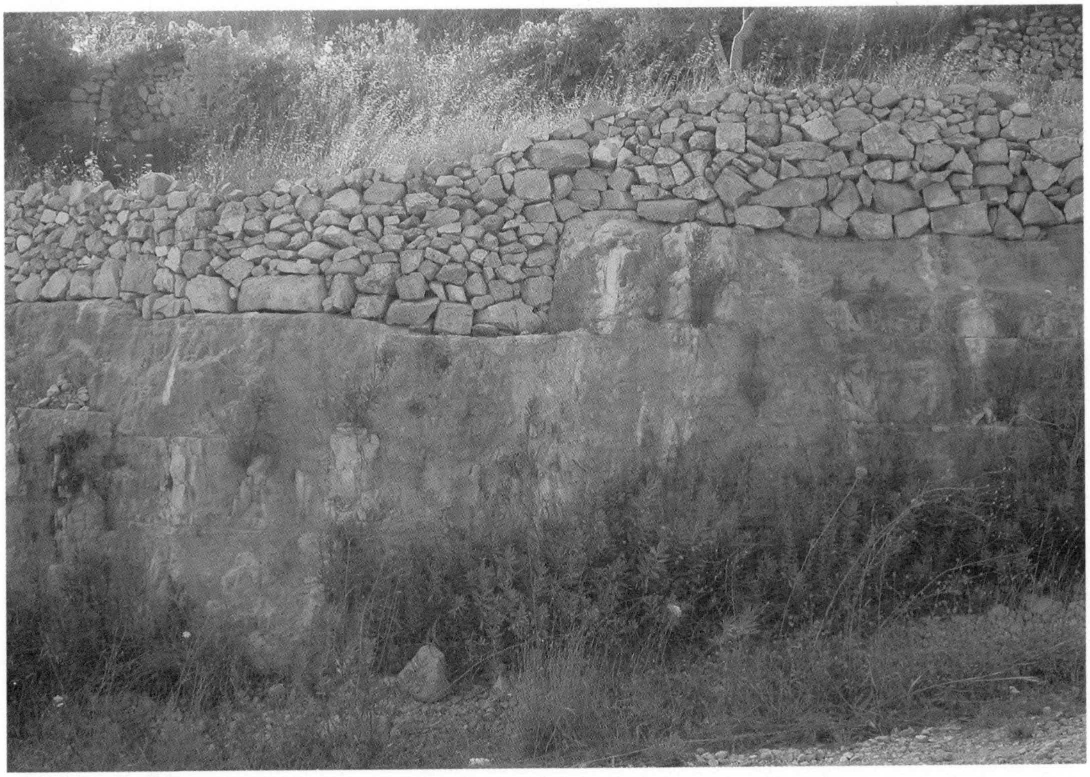

eventually led to dangerous physical limits that shatter the obvious joy the author experiences in the landscape—the eight metre concrete walls, the razor-wire fences, the military detention centres, hilltop fortresses of illegal settlers armed with the latest US small arms weaponry and their sniper dugouts, the camouflaged military bases. The limits of what are physically passable segue into the limits of what is verbally possible, of what is, in truth, unspeakable. It is thereby through these daily runs and the author's conversations with graciously hospitable local Palestinians met on the way, that we grasp the extent of what Mannes-Abbott describes as the "abusive non-sense" that cripples daily life by an Occupation that knows no limits. So too, if one were to try running in Khalil Rabah's pair of worn-in right-footed shoes, one would not get far.

Overstepping the limits of everyday Palestinian life, Mannes-Abbott encounters a militarised spatial domination and ownership that would be pathological if its 'logic' were not so transparently to force an autochthonous people from their land. Alas, Europeans have been the architects of such darkly barbaric spaces before. In this regard, Olaf Nicolai's introduction into Ramallah of Freud's text, *Mourning and Melancholia*, is particularly apposite. The histories of colonisation demonstrate that the shock of violent dispossession sets in motion a catastrophic mutilation of social structures and identities, in which the colonised self is deprived of a ground from which to narrate itself in the world and imagine new possibilities of existence. Najwan Darwish rightly describes it as "a kind of coma that the victim goes into, until he or she feels no pain". Scarred by traumatic inertia, retreating into nostalgia for an uncorrupted past, it commonly takes a people two or more generations to work through this state of melancholic loss to begin the reparative work of mourning. Darwish is of a generation that can see more clearly how "we should have resisted the colonial designs on our identity and memory"; but unhappily, in a state of psychic shock and physical weakness, collective unity and clarity of vision are rarely possible.

Nonetheless, Mannes-Abbott's running discloses a crucial psychological anchor for Palestinians to grasp tenaciously; namely, that ownership of space does not confer belonging to place. Place is produced in a reciprocal evolution of ecology with people—their pastoral and agricultural, linguistic and cultural practices. As the Palestinian filmmaker Maryse Gargour titled her 2008 documentary film, *The Land Speaks Arabic*, a language whose inflections are closest to Ugaritic, the most ancient language discovered in the territory.[4] In a poem, Mahmoud Darwish speaks of "the invaders' fear of memories", because the memories of the indigenous, embedded in land, language and culture, present a challenge to the legitimacy of the colonial narrative. It is in this sense that memorialising place becomes a weapon against the intruder, to which Mannes-Abbott's book too is testimony. However much the coloniser might try to appropriate or eradicate the signs of place (names, history, people, cuisine, the very ecology—and renaming in particular is 'entitlement', the first step to claiming property rights to a territory), it can never appropriate its fundamental nature; it can only concrete over it.... Is this intimate relation of language to place what is alluded to in Mark Titchner's photographs of words that merge with or recede into the surface of the stony ground? Although the words are English, they translate Palestinian sentiments. At least one discernable phrase—echoing the reference in Mannes-Abbott's text—is borrowed from a Mahmoud Darwish poem: "In/on this earth there is something to live for".

Perceived space, as Lefebvre insisted, is *produced* by its users; there is no *a priori* emptiness waiting to be filled. *Terra nullius* is the spurious pretext by which ruthless colonisers have justified ethnic cleansing and genocide since the Puritans claimed native America as their own God-given "promised land": a "desert", no less, to be reclaimed as Eden through agriculture, and which had to be freed of "strangers", "even if each mile is a marsh of blood".[5] As Segal and Steinback aptly comment, the Puritans "discovered" America not as an inhabited geography but through *scripture*: "the Puritan documents show the astonishing capacity of myth not only to obscure but to invent reality".[6] One does not need to overstate the obvious correspondence: Palestine was to be a place emptied of indigenous meaning then resold as mythified commodity. The "Biblical theme park" is an obvious sign; but aren't also the "synthetic worlds", as Mannes-Abbott aptly describes them, of illegal settlements, the Wall, the checkpoints, all the other structures of surveillance that spectacularise the land as a Zionist panopticon, in which the imprisoned residents, deprived of their own vistas, are not allowed to "look back"?

For the visitor the Separation Wall presents the most spectacularised sign of an unspeakable injustice.[7] For the Palestinians it offers one of the few surfaces on which they can register their contempt, most

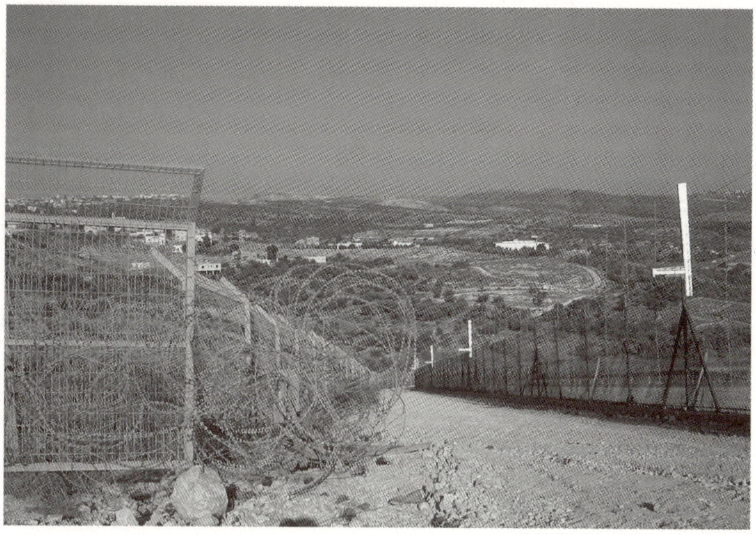

Occupation infrastructure; inside land-confiscating 'wall' at Bil'in, armaments on the ground where protestors have died, all well within the Green Line. Photography copyright Guy Mannes-Abbott.

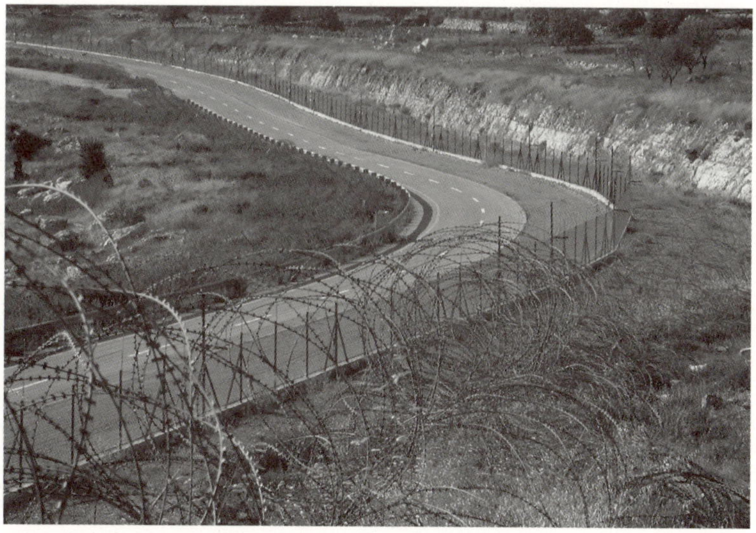

Occupation infrastructure; patrol road to the west of and below old Beitunia. Photography copyright Guy Mannes-Abbott.

famously on that section of the Wall that runs by Qalandia, once Jerusalem's airport, now a notorious checkpoint—although this has also become a site for graffiti tourists like Banksy.[8] Other surfaces tell their own stories. A tellingly different relation of space to surface than that of al-Ani's village murals was revealed by those painted by Jewish settlers on their side of the Wall 'protecting' the illegal Gilo settlement: a 'utopian' view of the overlooked landscape omitting all signs of the Palestinian town in the valley below. It is the impaired vision of Narcissus, reflecting the hollowness of a self devoid of any relation with an Other. Illegal settlements are 'conceived' spaces: fortified artifices produced not organically in relation to the land, but prefabricated by ideology and the logic of militaristic geometry and joined up by concrete networks to Israel's commercial centres. In these highways, as in the Gilo mural, the Palestinian Other is not seen; he has already been 'disappeared'. Of Paul Noble's pencil drawings, *This is The Way* conveys some sense of this alien geometry, presenting a parallelogram voided of any of the surrounding detail. *Family as Infinity (or Hard Labour)* however, presents a more ambiguous image that—like so much of the contents of the book—invokes what James Joyce called "two thinks at a time". On the one hand, the strange cubic edifice—crowned with loops of metal rising above a landscape populated with clusters of little stony 'dwellings'—recalls an illegal settlement. On the other, the structure is reminiscent of buildings in refugee camps, whose rooftops are festooned with the iron rods of reinforced concrete because, if families need to expand living space, they can only do so by building upwards.

An equally ambiguous politics inscribes Francis Alÿs' book pages, referencing the Armistice "Green Line" of 1949—long since violated by Israel—and the Wall. They invite us to imagine an opulent gold-leafed Wall coursing through a denuded landscape: a fraudulent monument to colonial hubris—another narcissistic folly? One can imagine its golden surface shimmering in the light of a hot summer's day, not quite believable, another mirage. As a possible metaphor of ill-gotten, squandered resources, Alÿs' imagined Wall is reminiscent of Baroque churches in Mexico, where the colonial Spanish—having such a surplus of gold mined by their native slaves gold leafed every conceivable interior surface. According to the UN, a shocking 45 per cent of international aid to Palestine ultimately supports the Israeli economy. Rather than hold Israel to account for human rights abuses, international aid organisations keep paying for the repair of infrastructures damaged by Israel, thereby absolving it of responsibility and sustaining its "deluxe Occupation".[9] From this perspective, Alÿs' Golden Wall is a resonant counterpoint to Mannes-Abbott's surprise at how, in a certain light, "Ramallah's business-like face looks like El Dorado" when seen from one of its hills. Myth and desire weight heavily in this landscape where even the ugly concrete of Occupation assumes a golden glow under the setting sun.

The issue of squandered resources returns us to the question of Ramallah. By arcing out towards its hinterlands, Mannes-Abbott subtly confirms Adania Shibli and Najwan Darwish's response to it as a city numbingly hollowed out of meaning for the national aspirations of Palestinians themselves, and described by many as a "bubble" insulated from realities in the West Bank and Gaza.[10] A city of promises, whose very administrative structure, engineered by Western 'interests', ensures they can never be fulfilled. In this place Mannes-Abbott is compelled to say that if he were a Palestinian "the world would keep turning without me".

In the streets of Ramallah one comes across Khaled Hourani's blue enamelled wall plaques with the Arabic and English legend "Jerusalem 14.63 km"; so near, and yet so far. Space metamorphoses into infinitely extendable time, so that, for a Palestinian even with the correct papers, a journey that once took 15 minutes can now take over three hours. In the autumn of 2010 the visitor may also have come across Al Riyadh, public billboards by Emily Jacir and Yazid Anani mimicking corporate construction site ads, which were part of the Municipality's *Wein a Ramallah* (Let's go to Ramallah) Festival.[11] One billboard, "Al-Riyadh Tower", depicted a fictional Dubai-like skyscraper; the other, "Al-Riyadh Villas" (albeit vandalised), a fictional settlement-style gated community. Legends in Arabic questioned what effects such corporate developments would have on the socio-economic structure of Ramallah; whether economic segregation exacerbates the fragmentation of Palestinian society initiated by the Occupier's physical fragmentation of land. Indeed, Mannes-Abbott's running takes him to the new suburban developments towards Ain Qiniya that already demarcate a neighbourhood of the wealthier Ramallah residents. As he says of one such development, "If it's indistinguishable from the work of the Occupation with its illiterate disinterest in the place and abstract construction of space, then is it Palestinian at all?"

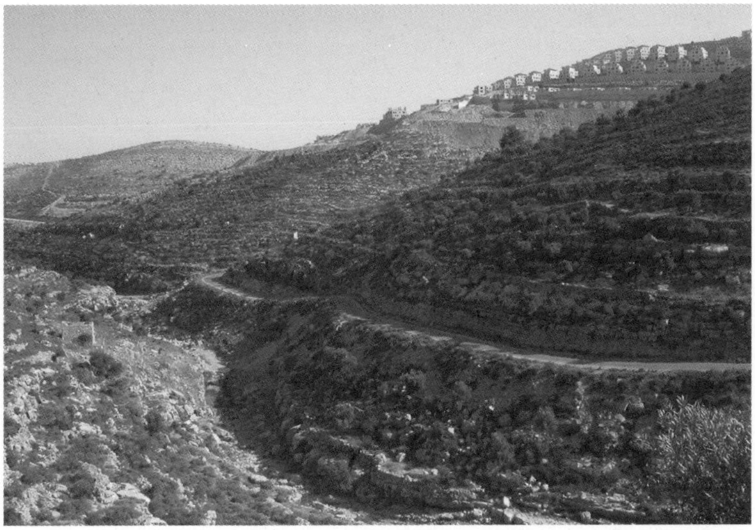

Wadi, qasrs, Roman spring, settler road (463), and Palestinian development on the ridge linked to Surda, north of Ramallah. Photography copyright Guy Mannes-Abbott.

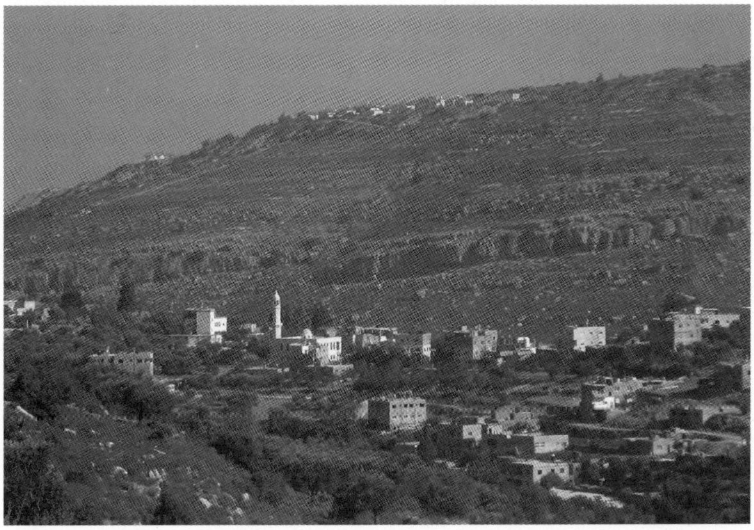

Ain Qiniya, over seen by the edge of Talmon settlement high on the ridge, Dolev's watchtower is out of frame to the left. Photography copyright Guy Mannes-Abbott.

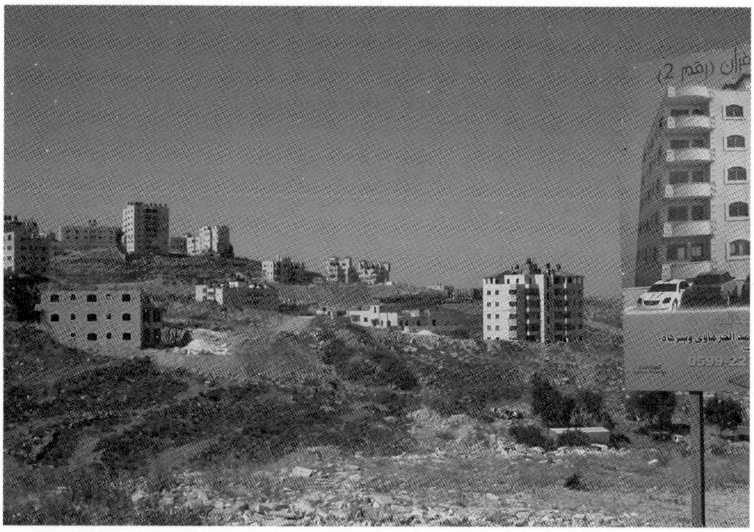

Occupation sanctioned Palestinian development at Beitunia. Photography copyright Guy Mannes-Abbott.

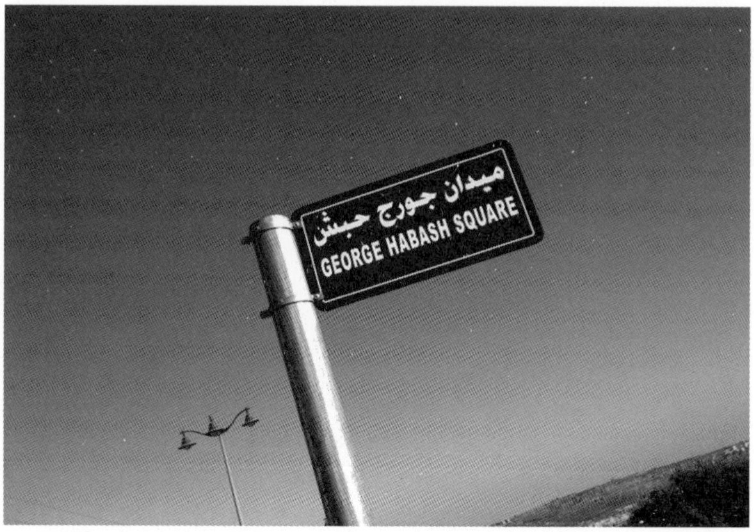

The 'missing' sign at George Habash Square; standing up before illegal settlements beyond. Photography copyright Guy Mannes-Abbott.

The *Wein a Ramallah* Festival was a culmination of the Municipality's Ramallah Centennial Project, inaugurated in 2006 to "revive a city that has been deteriorating due to the effects of more than 40 years of occupation." Among the cultural aims listed are "the promotion of tourism and investment", the motivation, one presumes, for introducing street names in Arabic and English (funded by USAID) and development of public space, including "George Habash Square", to which Mannes-Abbott's running persistently returns. "George Habash", however, is a name that conjures up the tantalising question: what if Palestine's negotiators had refused the terms of the Oslo Accords, of which Darwish is so bitterly critical?[12]

Since Palestine's means to build an independent economy is crippled by land seizure and export restrictions, the pressure on the Palestinian Authority to develop private sector programmes comes from foreign 'humanitarian' and 'developmental' aid organisations, overseen by the Quartet. But by late 2008 a coalition of aid agencies were already complaining that the Quartet were miserably failing in all its mandated humanitarian goals, with "partial achievement" in three of the "least pressing" areas: "securing donor pledges", "supporting Palestinian security reform" and "stimulating private sector activity".[13] In a book review, David Cronin relates how one of Envoy Blair's "quick impact projects"—providing market advice to Palestinian exporters—proved useless, "given that Blair was not prepared to use his platform as an international 'peace' envoy... to demand that Israel lift restrictions which prevented Palestinian firms from exporting goods in the first place".[14] If this is the reality then, as Anani and Jacir's billboards asked, for whom and to what purpose are the city's new high-rise corporate developments? In this context Rabah's shoes also take on added significance. We begin to see them as charity-shop donations from international NGOs, in which to focus on "humanitarian aid" is to hobble indefinitely Palestinian *political* aspirations for freedom and self-determination. Indeed, it is now clear to all that the 'Peace Process' has been a time-wasting sham, a "one-state, two-state" *pas de deux*, as Sharif Waked imagines it, in which two figures joined, then separated, finally coalesce in an uneasy embrace.

The Quartet's neoliberal displacement of political meaning by economic meaninglessness emerges as barely disguised social engineering designed to weaken not only traditional Palestinian affiliations, but also to entrench Israeli panoptical control by proxy. Darwish describes it as "an attempt to invent a new kind of Palestinian, a Palestinian without history and without memory, all for the benefit of the history and memory of the coloniser". It is to this that Ramallah's urban regeneration suspiciously bears witness. In an interview, Yazid Anani relates an example from Ramallah Municipality's regeneration plans. Al-Manara Square, established in 1905 under Ottoman control, had a strategic position and radial design, which enabled "whoever controlled it to dictate the transaction of imagery, symbolism, meanings and spatial politics"; as a social space it also became the focus for political rallies. However, in 1967 the Israeli Military Administration transformed it into a panoptical system prohibiting its use for political assembly, and this function has never been restored.[15] Instead, Ramallah's municipal plans include redesigning "al-Manara Plaza" for improved traffic flow by relocating pedestrians, out of sight, underground.[16] Inevitably, one asks where the 'busy' traffic is heading in this place, where, as Mannes-Abbott discovers, "life spirals within abysmal limits"?

Emily Jacir evokes an analogous movement in her "fragments of a diary". Here Palestine is never limited to geography but names an entire people, a majority trapped in refugee camps and waiting in limbo beyond the borders of their homeland, where "the cars circle / around and around / never reaching their destination / never finding their way home...." A complementary image appears elsewhere in her text: She sits with Hasan and Zafer in New York's Union Square smoking their arghiles, "watching the world whirling around us". There are two responses to this: either, like Barghouti's birds, Jacir echoes Mannes-Abbott's comment that if he were a Palestinian "the world would keep turning without me". Or, one might see in this whirling world a vacuity whose unacknowledged, absented centre is indeed named "Palestine". It is that to which all unanswered questions of human ethics, right and justice accrue, and for which a new generation is tasked with finding an imaginative resolution that neither forgets nor dwells in the past.

Ramallah, October 2010: In a long neglected garden stood a tiny pomegranate tree bearing two fruits. It must have seeded itself in this place with the aid of local birds. Like much revealed by Mannes-Abbott's running, it is an image of freedom, tenacity and survival in a ravaged landscape. As the Poet said, "We have on this earth what makes life worth living."[16]

Notes

[1] "Prison", Mourid Barghouti, *Midnight and Other Poems*, trans. Radwa Ashour, Introduction by Guy Mannes-Abbott, Lancs: Arc Publications, 2008, p. 216.

[2] In order to orientate myself relative to Mannes-Abbott's excursions, I went to Google Maps. Here one finds a pre-emptive delegitimisation of Palestine whose towns and cities are listed as "Ramallah, Israel"; "Nablus, Israel"; "Qalandia Refugee Camp, Jerusalem, Israel", and so forth; Gaza alone is designated "Palestinian Territories".

[3] Lefebvre, Henri, *The Production of Space*, trans. Donald Nicholson-Smith, Oxford, UK and Cambridge, MA: Blackwell, 1991.

[4] L Ra'ad, Basem, *Hidden Histories: Palestine and the Eastern Mediterranean*, London: Pluto Press, 2010. Ugaritic has been related to the Canaanite peoples who occupied the territory prior to the Israelite invasions. Even were they true, Biblical claims of "Jewish ownership" do not morally justify or provide a legal basis for ethnic cleansing.

[5] Elder Palfrey to John Endicott, 1630s, quoted in Richard Drinnon, *Facing West: The Metaphysics of Indian-Hating and Empire-Building*, New York: New American Library, 1980, p. 4.

[6] M Segal, Charles and David C Steinback, *Puritans, Indians and Manifest Destiny*, New York: GP Putnam's Sons, 1977, p. 17.

[7] If the Wall's publicly stated rationale is to ensure Israel's 'security', not least for illegal settlements, a glance at the map of its course shows that its reality is to individually isolate Palestinian towns and villages and separate the people from their farmland, livelihoods and families. And yet the Wall is rather more easily dismantled than the concrete highways, prohibited to Palestinians, which also cut through their land depriving them of the resources to sustain a viable, independent economy.

[8] A further graffito—perhaps by yet another 'witty' tourist—has been added to Banksy's much-reproduced stencil of the girl floating upwards with balloons: a pen, carrying two further balloons, has written,"Sister you need more?", which sums up the hollowness of international aid to Palestine.

[9] Cronin, David, "New book shows how aid to PA ended up in Israel's pockets", *The Electronic Intifada*, 18 May 2011. Cronin reviews Sahar Taghdisi-Rad, *The Political Economy of Aid in Palestine: Relief from Conflict or Development Delayed?*, Oxon and New York: Routledge, 2011.

[10] One might equally call Tel Aviv a "bubble", wilfully blind to realities the 'other' side of the Wall.

[11] Al Riyadh was commissioned for an exhibition Ramallah—the Fairest of Them All?, curated by Vera Tamari and Yazid Anani, for the Ethnographic and Art Museum at Birzeit University in partnership with Ramallah Municipality's Wein a Ramallah Festival. An interview with Anani discussing his views on urbanisation in Ramallah was published at www.artterritories.net.

[12] George Habash, after being sidelined by Arafat in the PLO, founded the Popular Front for the Liberation of Palestine. A staunch nationalist, Habash advocated a one-state solution and believed the Oslo Peace Accords had sold out Palestinian interests. Given the extent to which Israel has since been allowed to confiscate Palestinian land towards creating an "Eretz Israel", one has to admit that, with respect to the Oslo Accords, he was not wrong.

[13] "Middle East Quartet is failing, warn aid agencies", http://www.savethechildren.org.uk/en/4_middle-east-quartet; accessed 30 May 2011. The issue of "supporting Palestinian security reform" is itself highly contentious, in so far as the Palestinian security authority is widely perceived as a proxy or subcontractor of Israel's security machine.

[14] Cronin, David, "New book shows how aid to PA ended up in Israel's pockets", 2011.

[15] Shuruq Harb, Interview with Yazid Anani, 7 September 2010, www.artterritories.net.

[16] Ramallah Municipality 2006–2010. Centennial Project booklet. www.ramallah.ps.

[17] Mahmoud Darwish, "On this Earth", in *Unfortunately, It Was Paradise: Selected Poems*, Berkeley: University of California Press, p. 6.

In Ramallah, Running

Guy Mannes-Abbott

I am running in Ramallah.

Running through, around and on Ramallah; hill of God, god of hills. Running almost 1,000 metres above Mediterranean Sea level, almost 1,000 feet further above Dead Sea level. Running on the seven hills that Ramallah is said, with radical understatement, to inhabit. Everything in Ramallah is a hill or hills in apparent infinity; up and down and up, sharply, severely, steeply, gently, deceptively, constantly. Everything between hills is becoming Ramallah, spreading, forging, declaiming the old and new, for now, forever?

Running connotes residence; a home being run from or to, one nearby. I'm making Ramallah homely by running here, leaving some of myself out there, drawing into myself whatever is here. Shortening and lengthening my time. Running is a proof of my existence, my proof that, as the poet wrote, "I exist." The essence of running involves "exerting yourself to the fullest within your individual limits" which is also a "metaphor for life"—according to the novelist. It doesn't sound like much, until you do it.

Running in Ramallah, I encounter things that are contradictory even conflicting but little I could describe as paradoxical. Despite its sweetly sophisticated humours this is not a place that can afford paradox.

I'm running in Ramallah and it is painful.

On Limits.

Freedom has limits and always works against them. Life is lived against its own limit; resisted, made fruitful or at least memorialised by these means. A life lived well is one lived in defiance of its limits. Surely, if freedom means anything to us, it is this experience of being alive as an opening out.

I'm in Ramallah, a place of compelling character set amongst elegantly bare hills and valleys of verdant fruitiness. It's the 'as if' capital of an 'as if' statelet that isn't even allowed its own land in Hollywood during Oscar season—and yet this is Palestine all right. Palestine is its people and their place, the two interwoven and anchored in the beginnings of human time. In our first port and earliest known city; Yaffa and Ariha/Jericho respectively.

I'm in Ramallah which became a city a century ago, when still a small town on the road from Jerusalem to Nablus. It grew in leaps; doubling after 1948, leaping again after 1967 and since 1995 has expanded over ridges to swallow neighbouring al Bireh and even Beitunia. Today the scale and rapidity of its development express the embrace of present limits on what it means to be Palestinian here. Spatially Ramallah is under military Occupation and surrounded by settlements which have been staged on as many hill tops as possible. It does not possess its own earth, air or water. Visually Ramallah is focusing inwards, growing itself a means of blocking off the view of occupiers and usurpers. However, this screen of development also removes its own view out, of the plains, villages and ancestral homes of '48 Palestine. For now this is how it is.

In Ramallah forms of vibrant life survive to a remarkable extent. If you look you will see it with the arrival of morning light; as coffee is cooked up, breads baked, vegetables made upstanding downtown, as people from surrounding villages settle with their fruits and herbs and men fill the cafés as they always have. Standing outside the Palestine Café, Murad breaks off from his friend to tell me that he's from Jifna, home of the "mishmish" or short-seasoned Apricot, a few kilometres north. That his name means 'priest', which he repeats three times while his equally elderly friend tugs at his head-dress; "holy man!"

As the light fades a more exclusively Ramallah vibrancy opens up on front stoops and terraces, in the municipal park and open-air bars. If you listen you will hear where the limits of life run out; hard-to-breath stories about blue and green identities, linked to the real difficulty of going anywhere more than a few kilometres south, east or west, running gauntlets to go a bit further north. Limits everywhere, inexplicable, horribly close, definitive of life here and policed with mortal consequence.

I'm in Ramallah witnessing how there is no freedom for the people or what remains of the place. How its people have taken strong possession of themselves to stretch and adapt to living without freedom with singular and humbling effect, but coming up against the reality of what it actually means at every turn. "In/on this earth", wrote the poet, "there is something to live for." What? It can only be the breaching of these limits, to be in reach of a "blue peninsula" of potential life, the simple freedom to live as you will.

I wanted to discover the limits to what this means. Not the limits of freedom because there is none here, but of "this earth", of what there is "to live for", of that "something" itself. That "something to live for" is the freedom to work against these very limits, to have a meaningful life. Here as elsewhere walking embodies life's freedom, it is the shortest route to experiencing it. Walking enacts freedom, so I decided to walk.

In Ramallah walking soon reaches the limits, not merely of the city but the limits of life itself. At the same time Ramallah is doing a good job of putting any such limits out of its mind, to focus instead on that something in the present, life as it is for now—amongst variously enriched interiors. And without walking. Ramallese describe this as a syndrome, life here as a bubble. I wanted to encounter one of the actual limits, to walk in one direction until I reached a physical limit and could walk no more. I'm a bubble-burster by temperament but well aware that my freedom is expressed or indulged by my presence here.

So I set off from my hilltop refuge on a street signed "Al Jihad (Struggle) Street", via a vertiginous zigzag of new roads below and aiming for a small village called Rafat. At least, from the confusion of maps redefined with imprisoning features, endless new names, attributions and legal limits manifested in massive earthworks or concrete flanks, gigantic deforming infrastructure and complex militarised zones, I think it's called Rafat and I believe I can reach it by following a seasonal river valley or *wadi* out from the city.

Topographically-speaking, the wadi descends southwards five kilometres from Ramallah's old town to Rafat although the first kilometre has long been expensively residential, the second very rapidly filling with banks of high-rises and massive Palestinian Authority Ministry buildings crowding its steep sides. Beyond them a lane trickles between terraced hillsides of twinned ridges stretching to the south, one topped by an unmanned Occupation watch post. At the moment the city stops abruptly here, nomadic Bedouin tend the weary terraces, their children's voices charm the silence.

Ahead is the unusually tall new minaret at Rafat and a larger than expected village banked up beyond a lush green valley of well maintained fig and olive trees. There is a peculiarly idyllic air down in this valley for the last kilometre before the village, despite the prison fencing with snarling razor wire up high on the westerly bank. As farmhouses loom through the trees I notice another camouflaged bunker; two storeys high and evidently manned with at least one figure tracing my approach. These soldiers are posted between Rafat and Ramallah, there's no point in asking why the villagers have become human shields. Or why I aim my camera through the leaves and shoot.

Expecting interdiction at any moment, I keep on towards the far edge of the village. As the track curls up I turn off into a foreshortened field, the rear of which is lined with prison-camp fencing and floodlights. The lights point in to the camp interior as per war movie and look starkly out of place here to me as yet. I expected something like this and walked here to find it but the crude actuality is shocking. Conscious of every snatched second, I cross quickly and stand below the lights and three to four metre high razor wire coils running into the distance. Beyond is an unnaturally neat road with immaculate storm drains, further lined with electrified fencing on a wide strip of land stolen from Rafat village. Beyond that lies the notorious Ofer military detention centre not yet visible to me.

I'm moving hastily and don't immediately notice how it all links further south to a substantial gash in the landscape containing a dual carriageway, storming traffic and then a prettily disguised wall of concrete. Here at the limits is another world, hard to take in visually, harder to comprehend. I decide to follow the limits to the east and a rocky embankment just before the new mosque or *mas'jid.* I slip up through the village, greeting late afternoon terrace-gatherers and up to a rocky vantage point above the big road. Here is a clear view of its muscular thrust to the west, joining Jerusalem with the airport at historical Lydda, the 'cleansing' or *le-taher* of which generated a significant part of the '48-generation of refugees in Ramallah to this day.

I stand on the rocky hillside looking out beyond the forbidding and for Palestinians forbidden motorway. These are the real limits, what limits of this kind mean. Go no further, you cannot get out. In fact you can barely see out at the life that is freely here on this land and nor are you meant to. This massively defended road and invasive cutting is built on recently confiscated farmland owned by the people of Rafat. Rafat is a Canaanite name dating to about 3,000 years and has Roman ruins in the village. Many similarly ancient olive trees were sacrificed for the road, while the entire area confiscated for roads, walls, prison fences, the military camp to the west and its security infrastructure amounts to about 40 per cent of historic Rafat.

Standing here on exposed rock I am unaware of these facts, not thinking about figures. I'm thinking that these are the limits of everything that matters, that even looking seems futile. For the people of Rafat there may be something worth living for in or on what remains of this land but many won't live long enough to experience it. Limits like this link generations here in ways and severity that is surely unique.

Back in Ramallah, I mention walking to Rafat and The Birdman tells me for the first time of someone living in the village with a strong resemblance to me. If it were me, I'd be forced to live out my entire life within this imprisoning limit with no hope of end, remission or access to justice. The world would keep turning without me. The absoluteness of this sentence is another unique characteristic of these limits.

My eyes drift to the dried ears of grass blowing daintily in the wind before my haunched knees. On this earth there is something to live for and it is not this. These limits are not generative in any philosophical or poetic way. They lack justice of course, but also sense. This is how it is for now. Standing here is not how I expected it to be; not obvious or banal but disturbingly, insistently particular. I thought there was nothing I could add, now I'm not sure there are words for it—which is different.

Life is so resilient in Rafat that it has found something to live for, even if it means little without breaching these limits. It is on the earth beyond that life has abandoned meaning to the abstract non-sense of a brutal Occupation without limit. On the earth over there every possibility exists, but I'm not sure it's something to live for. I don't think it counts. In any case, it's less than this.

I'm running in Ramallah, but not for long.

Running extends my residency; it works slowly by taking me to places I would not otherwise go, repeatedly. It works fast by taking me to many places as quickly as Google, but concretely. I've been there, been back and can go again in no time. Running discourages thinking or conclusion, concentrates on the present. The present is what is, how things are for now. I'm running in the present and peculiarly alive to the details of what is around me.

Running down I pass teams of builders arriving on site. I run out on the main road into yellow taxi-busses or *servees*, UN-badged 4x4s, mothers driving children to school and again on our return loops. Running through Bat'n al Hawa, the road is up; work not underway until I return, an object of mirth, recognition and warm encouragement. Westerly panoramas once began here but the view is now of trench work and substrata, the spraying of sticky tarmac one day, a smooth new surface another. At the end is Zamn, beacon of up town Ramallah, which opens at downtown hours but their coffee is weak, expensive.

On deluxe al Tireh Street I settle into my rhythm and watch police guards changing shifts along the newly mansioned ridge which leads to the city's north-west extremity. I pass them standing armed in groups of four at junctions along the way, offer greetings, share smiles.

Passing me they do the same. When I reach the city's new panoramas at the end of the ridge today, four soldiers stand guard with muscles, big guns and a matching jeep. We amuse each other before I step aside to look out myself, begin the run back in to town. Overtaking me on al Tireh's incline, each waves an individual greeting to the cliché I embody, the joke that I get, the ambiguity of the fact that it is me that is running.

When I am not running I'm thinking, details stack up. The present acquires depth and dimension, things become complex. They change; everything. I am one of very few people in Ramallah who can prove their existence merely by running in the hills. One of few here who don't need to exert themselves to the utmost just to prove that they exist.

I'm the only person I see who is running in Ramallah.

Off Limits.

Histories of Ramallah describe how a handful of families bought land from al Bireh village to found the city 450 years ago. It's gone on to swallow up al Bireh, which still retains the airs and dormitory quiet of a village. It opens up late and residents boast of being in the country, though visual distinctions are less clear to me.

One thing that is clear in al Bireh is the view from every window of the alien settlement atop the hill immediately to its east; Jabal al Tawiil. While Ramallah has almost succeeded in blocking out the view of this fortified intrusion, al Bireh lies beneath it. The poet wrote of his horror at first seeing it, an architect shows me walls restored before missiles from it damaged them again, others speculate about dismantling the most symbolic of all settlements which brought American militants via the Sinai in 1981; early 'peace' dividends.

I want to walk around the stolen hill to discover what is beyond, naively curious about what happens at the limits. The settlement appears to have turned its back on the city, the people and place to look out over hills that form one of the Occupation's military zones. The settlement itself is now well-mapped, but the hill immediately to the east of it is harder to fathom since the only guide is an outdated Google Earth. I'm hoping to climb it so that I can overlook the settlers and see the view east that they have stolen.

I arrive at al Waled's in the heart of the vegetable market before the chickpeas have even been ground, depart along al Mudarris Street towards the big mas'jid. Nearby Jabal al Tawiil Street bears a weathered sign on an antique building, bends around a cemetery as it rises eastwards. The settlement looms imposingly; an ugly military apparatus of wall, wire, watchtowers, lights and barracks. Confusingly, the flanks of the hill are home to expensive-looking new developments between established residential quarters right up to the forbidding rear gate of the settlement. Of course, it is the settlers who have encroached upon residents of the place.

Before I get close I'm warned off by two passing vehicles; the second actually reverses back to make sure I've understood that it's too dangerous to do what I'm attempting. "You cannot go around there, they shoot down there sometimes. There's a checkpoint and they'll stop you anyway, but don't go; it's dangerous for you to go", Rami explains. He's a self conscious dude so his effort to offer sober detail and advice is impressive and I assure him that I'll take his word to the top of the road and not loop the hill.

At the top, concrete blocks and the steel of Occupation crowd a disused gate linked to the military base inside, beside which are inhabited homes. Parallel with the high security fence is a residential road, one of whose startled residents invites me in and up to his terrace with its revealing views. Saleh explains even more methodically about the dangers of my plan, looking concerned enough to master emotion for more convincing effect. "They throw things, they are shooting from up there. No, no, they will stop you, they, *yanni*, anything happens here, anything can happen. They're shooting from the hill at us; it's too dangerous", he says. This is not fear; he confides and condemns, but his sense is clear.

I'm tempted to tell him a white lie when I leave. Despite his bafflement at my appearing to downplay the perils he lives with, I cannot just give in. So I find the road that loops around the back of the hill, the sides of which are still terraced as most of the hill was before being stolen, field by field. High up above is a security fence with giant lights but no more watchtowers or sign of cameras so I walk on, alone, calmly, silently primed.

As the road descends dumper trucks climb towards me. White plated, they're Palestinian and we wave at each other cheerily. At the lowest point in the rubble and rubbish strewn lane is a small hut beside a classic checkpoint; concrete blocks with a heavy metal barrier. Inside, a small fat man is bent over with face obscured, chattering to himself in Hebrew. I'm tempted to keep walking but decide to offer my smile rather than my back. He smiles too, indeed, stands with an unnervingly fixed grimace whilst instructing me with a firm arm to go that way, up there, go up the hill. I have no choice, but know he's sending me to settlement security. I climb a faltering path, looking back on his insistent arm.

A road at the top reveals the settlement surrounded by security infrastructure fit for a small airport. Neat suburban houses crowd the easterly slope, above a classic two-way security gate and a homely ramp for tank access. Only a few years ago Ramallah was reinvaded by 150 tanks and APCs, an unimaginable thought. Ahead is only trouble. As I walk slowly towards it I realise that the hill I was hoping to find now looms to my left. Alluringly bare, it wears a meandering pathway on its far edge, the beginning of which is opposite the settlement's gates. I step calmly over and keep walking on up the hill without glancing back or taking a breath. I've got to try it.

I climb steadily but cannot shake a sickening degree of anxiety which is also fitting given what I know to be true.

It's only days since nine people were killed on the Mavi Marmara (part of an aid flotilla for Gaza in International waters), forcing on the world a glimpse of everyday reality here inside the Occupation. I know the well-documented history of shootings and massacres, the bottomless impunity of soldiers and settlers. Settlers who are watching, perhaps readying to shoot me now as I walk up a hill that I'm forbidden to approach. I feel exceedingly exposed to their mercy; a very strange sensation. I step to the highest point of the track, hoping they might have the decency to shoot me in the legs. Realise they don't but that—like so many children, passers-by, protesters before me—I will not hear the explosion in my head. Then that I'd miss my new-found runner's legs; it wouldn't be worth it.

I am not being heroic, nor exaggerating or debunking. I've looked down the barrel of many an automatic, been caught-up in no-mans-land on many warring borders, feared for my life in Honduran fields, witnessed state sponsored massacres in Gujarat, India, but even these things are exceptions and retained some legibility. Here it happens all the time, every day and for decades on end. If they fancy shooting me in the head, they will. There is no way to calibrate the risk involved in continuing to walk here on the hill, or imagine what the back of my head looks like to a mad gunman on a stolen hill. It makes for a unique anxiety and matching relief when I reach the far side of the hilltop out of sight of the settlement. It's a matter of being able to breath again.

Wadis open out and curl away with characteristic elegance, the dump is far below but right in front of me are two concrete sniper points with camouflage nets. I stand in each slowly, carefully, looking out at what they were built to shoot at; the Palestinian dump workers on one side, scattered Palestinian homes across

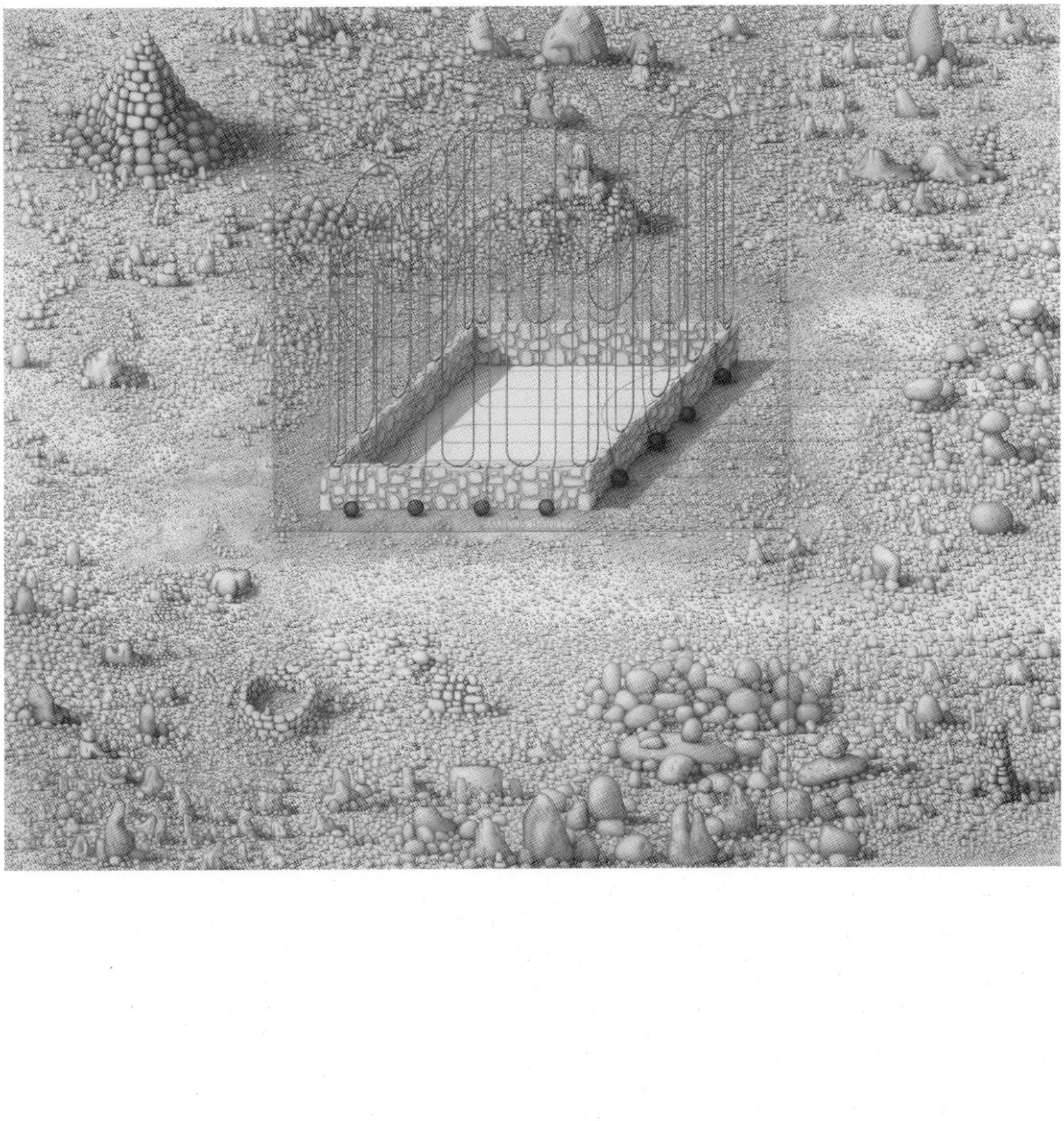

the valley on the other. This hill and the equally bare-sided ones that dominate views east and south are all within so-called "Area C"; land annexed by the Occupation often categorised as a military zone and rendered white on maps. Above distant folds I can see settler outposts with their classic caravans clustered around communication masts. To the west, not only can I not see Ramallah, it might as well not exist. Meanwhile I'm standing on sniping grounds, clambering around military assets central to the settler's world view.

I circle the hilltop until the twee suburban estate on Jabal al Tawiil lies opposite me. I'm trying not to look in any sustained way but to check if anyone is there, or a group forming to take me down. Instead I'm concentrating wilfully on my dusty feet; low bushes of prickly *natsh* amid rocky outcrops, wiry green thistles and the smaller blue-purple versions that hug the ground. At one point half a metre of snake flashes between them. At another, three Fallow deer see me and dart off in a panic, bottoms bouncing as they zigzag for their lives.

I drop behind the highest rock I've yet seen and take surveying photographs so that I can stare later. They reveal a classic settler stage set; red roofed, unnaturally neat white villas, most with shutters firmly closed to the view. An industrial chimney and communication masts covered in aerials of varying kinds tower over it all. Settlement began at the northern end, declining towards the south-east where newer villas are more spaced out, before lowering to clusters of new immigrants in standard issue white caravans with recently acquired Israeli flags. These house Russian militants, who are most vulnerable in their new homeland and most aggressive in defending their subsidised presence. In all the photographs there is not a single person outside even in the cool part of the morning. Perhaps that is why I'm telling the tale.

Walking down the hill I concentrate on occasional tiny bright yellow flowers on my path, start to feel like I've got away with it; that I can reach the road and walk round the hill back to Ramallah. At that moment a big roar sends an APC up the road towards the bend where this pathway ends. I slow but don't stop, knowing how it works here. I've been spotted, they've sent for the military and now it will be very boring. It roars to a near halt, pang. Without actually stopping it revs hard, sticks to the road and roars off. It returns within no time, pang, does exactly the same thing. Perhaps the pangs are the point.

At the junction I resort to shadows and notice a quaint sign through layers of wire of a sweetly bucolic, *innocent* idea of a communal village: P'sagot. It looks positively fascistic standing before the concrete blocks, tank ramp and ruined Palestinian terraces. I turn away and down a perfectly straight road with motorway lights on the side open to the hills. Rolls of razor wire extend the bank above me, little red roofs visible above that. I stick to the sheltering rock as yellow-plated vehicles drive lividly fast down the road, others flash up it without my granting them notice. It's unnerving; I expect one to stop and ask me what I'm doing, the prelude to the kind of trouble I've avoided thus far. The prelude for a Palestinian to routine arrest, violence or murder—like the boy shot last week by a settler on a road linked to this 15 kilometres north.

Halfway along cars dry up and the view to the south opens to hilly flanks that delight my eye. The sight of these mounds which hide their secrets so well in aridity always fills me with the pleasures of aesthetic possession, illegitimate pride. I cross the road to see closer, and within a few steps notice a bullet lying beside the tarmac. Not any old bullet or shotgun cartridge, but a large bright brassy new one; seven centimetres long, tapering to an elegant point. I reach to pick it up and feel its heat before restoring its explosive form to the ground beside a rusty neighbour on the roadside opposite the settlement. Later I check; these bullets are top of the range snipers' munitions, used by the best equipped American forces. Abu Q teases me for not hanging one around my neck, like the *shabab*, but then he's a poet and values his aging fingers as much as I do.

I've had enough and want to get out of here. Snipers' shelters, jumping deer, live munitions roadside, combine with years of well archived facts freshened up by last week's haul of like-minded foreigners at sea. As if on cue cars start racing by again. Now I do look at the faces of each solitary driver, who don't look back. What can be in their minds? I pass a road sign in Hebrew, and start to hope that beyond the bend materialising as expected there is a loop back to safe Palestinian ground. At the bend I climb away from the road to absorb the astonishing view. A deep wadi lowers further between perfectly massed Palestinian hills. At the top is the one I've reclaimed; a perfect rounded form, lovely horizontal strata, detailed with that seductive aridity.

Up ahead the settler road curls back again and continues into the distance for as far as I can see. At the s-bend stands a typical Occupation watch tower under a big flag. I have no idea how I can get back if I cannot do as I had hoped and walk on anxiously. A burnt-back hillside opposite the watchtower would allow me to climb back but the soldiers inside probably won't. The something inside me has now become indignation. Then I spot a sewage plant, significantly lower than the settler road on its far left side; settler shit! In place of a return path? I keep on; hopeful, anxious, pissed-off.

Suddenly, and to my intense relief, below the road to my right appears another thin track which I quickly decide is the one I could see on Google Earth, my only guide to these forbidden zones. I can get back! Filled with something like time traveller elation, I speed up, desperate for human warmth and conversation with people who stand on this earth and humble before it. As I'm wondering how to get down a truck appears and then stops, having seen me high above. It reverses back up out of the road tunnel and I start wondering again. But it's plates are definitely white: Palestinian! I'm safe and the driver is shouting to me, I think, something about Jerusalem. I'm just figuring out how to get down the steep slope and then just dive into a slide down it.

"Got to get back to Ramallah!" I say, before recognising Rami, my old friend from a couple of hours ago.

He asks how I got here.

"On the settler road, don't know how, but...."

I'm thinking that all those cars, drivers, watchers must have found my appearance ambiguous enough to let me pass. It must have seemed more likely that I was visiting a mad religious aunt from Brooklyn—hence out walking—than doing what I was doing; being, in essence, their enemy. Rami is weighing the same thought, swallowing his own small anxiety. It re-emerges as we sit around a makeshift table of crates and bricks with his colleagues from al Bireh's sewage works and settle down to Palestinian breakfast.

Breads are handed around, pots of things opened up, hands dive through invitations to eat, jokes about any hint of hesitation, before more food is thrust into my hands. Warm, generous, intensely relaxing for me—not so simply for them. There is still something inexplicable about my having defied advice to walk around there and return on the settler road. More than one fellow diner has been imprisoned without charge, since when their lives have been restricted to this hilly prison. The bottom line is that if I do things like this and get stopped with something that identifies them on me too, then anything can and does routinely happen—to them, not me. So no photographs, no real names.

Rami and his younger helper drop me near the mas'jid in al Bireh. We part unsentimentally but as they drive away goats spill into al Ain Street, diverting traffic and drawing their suitably country-dressed minder behind them. It's a reminder of the place that I set out from and have returned to; that which exists over time, maturing, altering sedimentally, accommodating all the strange wonders of this city amongst the hills.

In contrast, the fort on Jabal al Tawiil exists only as space; place in time, time in place. A place, this place, but not for long. When it's gone, nothing will remain of the space it is in the place that it was and will be. Meanwhile, settlers hide up there in their synthetic 'world' behind shuttered windows and gun sights. For the time being they can shoot high-end sniper bullets at will at anyone they don't like the look of. For now they occupy abstract space and this is what they have chosen to do with their time here. The zone of irreality exclusive to these settlers is not at the limits nor merely beyond them, it is off-limits.

Today I wandered off-limits too, but found my way back. Did walking embody or enact my freedom or freedom as such? No, it was a walk powered by naiveté and relative privileges; white skin, ambiguous physical appearance, luck—as several trusted people reiterate in the coming days—and my not knowing instinctively how limits work here. The hour of the day played a part too. My reward, which gains dimension in coming days, is sufficient direct experience to know that I would not attempt it again. Today walking enacted my good fortune at getting back to Ramallah with legs intact.

In Ramallah, I'm running in the clouds.

I open my door at seven to passing wisps and trails rushing in as if someone were spraying it at me. The sound of quite heavy traffic signals normality, so I set out left, then right and down, left, right and right on the main road down towards Yaffa Street, left down and up sharply, then start to run uphill against the traffic.

Running along Bat'n al Hawa towards al Tireh Square I can see out west to Khirbat al Tireh—the ruins or remains of Roman through Byzantine eras—and the top of the minaret buried in the suburb on the far side of the ridge easily enough. It's clearing now, no more fragmentary cloud only misty haze. Even that clears as the sun starts to hit, hotly. At the end an elderly man speed-walking in running gear replies in American English to my greeting in Arabic.

I'm running slowly and in my own time, managing not to borrow momentum from the slopes. I tackle inclines steadily, watching each foot fall in front of the other as interest accrues in my knees. Past friendly guards outside the Chinese Embassy, al Huda's gas station above the new minaret on Salah'ddin Street and on. In each direction police people carriers race up and down, lights silently flashing, always in threes. It's not far to the junction which rounds off current development at the end of the ridge, beyond which a road drops into the wadi below. George Habash Square is named after the least compromised leader of a liberation party. It offers a seductive view on this perfect morning.

Standing still, my eyes run over curvy flanks dotted with olive trees and stone built refuges, hills beyond in difficult to separate out rolls and rounds, ghostly radio masts. Mid-horizon is a hill with buildings clustered under trees, above a deep wadi with scattered dwellings that must be Ain Qiniya, a small village beyond the grid. Beside it a hill is scarred by a track leading to a cleared area on top. Beyond that a fine towering hill is tipped with confections in white and red. Alongside, grand ridges stretch elegantly eastwards, flaunting the incisions and encrustations of new development. Gorgeous curves display the irregular lines of farmed terraces over the already pronounced horizontal strata that is Palestine's signature. Beyond nearby olive groves, hills darkened by morning light throw up mysterious silhouettes. Questions I will answer with my feet.

In Ramallah, I'm told the sea is visible on a clear day. Out over the plains of historical Palestine, you can see the ancient port of Yaffa—the harbour lights, perhaps even boats—at night. It's not far and entirely credible but so far all I've seen beyond the hilly detail of Ramallah's hinterland is a warm brown ocean of bubbling haze filling in all the valleys on the horizon. At first glance it resembles a stormy sea but I'm too much at home in the mountain air to believe my eyes.

Running in the clouds, Ramallah clarifies.

Within Limits.

Ramallah's northerly limit is a long wadi linking Surda in the east to Ain Qiniya in the west. It is part of an ancient route extending towards the coast at Yaffa, memorialised by Roman stonework at a spring far below the city. This wadi, whose name I never discover, has long marked the natural limit of the Hill of God—though nothing is natural or simple when it comes to limits in Ramallah.

The dry river bottom in the wadi is twinned by a road, route 463, linking Surda junction to Ain Qiniya and settlements beyond. I've been obsessed with the accessibility of the 463 for some time, though still not aware of its origins. Fascinated too by the village of Ain Qiniya and its connective wadi, especially having seen them from George Habash Square. Both ends of the wadi bore Occupation checkpoints until very recently. Surda's notorious checkpoint on the road to Birzeit and its university has been the subject of artworks and protests. It also generated a long hilly detour, which is how A's mother fell and broke her leg so badly that she is only standing on it now after more than three years. Ain Qiniya had a dedicated cluster of roadblocks and a checkpoint but their reported removal means it should now be 'open'.

I've been to Surda before, on a snatched attempt to walk the wadi. I walked north to the city's edge where I met Fahed, a resident of apartments overlooking the east end of the wadi. While we cut through back streets to show me clear directions, he explained that "down there is a closed area". I should keep on through Surda, then follow the road and track to the left; "it's a very long way", he said, offering to share the food he'd just bought. So I traversed the squiggling junction where the checkpoint had been and kept close to the brand new highway through Surda until I reached Abu Qash in the dusk. Along the way a farmer gave me some green plums which—together with unripened cherries—are popular here and intended to hydrate. Later I will understand how Ain Qiniya is accessible by such circuitous means, what Fahed meant by "closed area" and why he was mistaken.

Today I'm determined to reach Ain Qiniya and so follow my instincts at Surda's collision of roads. An unlikely candidate for a mapped road, the 463's narrow track falls steeply away from the big road between little fields and massed rubble, towering new suburbs at Surda and high-rises at Ramallah's northernmost extent. This derelict ravine is Fahed's "closed area" and several kilometres along it is peculiarly isolated Ain Qiniya. I have time to savour the walk before sun fall, though the climb back up to al Tireh and along the ridge doubles the prospect.

The first kilometre or two is dismaying however much I muster justification, explanations and cheeriness. The upside is that I've dropped out of the present; all the noise, new build and human energy above, into an enveloping stillness. To my left terraced hillsides climb dramatically to the edge of the city. My right is more abruptly covered by rocky cliffs over which a humble form of stone terracing levels out sloping rocks, fills gaps and bolsters the hillside around old olive trees. This loving hand labour of generations is impressive as well as simply beautiful. Where the sun hits the roadside, it ignites fierce odours of the wild sage that is drunk as tea. Armfuls of this potent weed together with seasonal berries like 'toot' seem to be the lowest point of entry at the downtown market.

Otherwise it's a hellish vision; a winding track lined on each side with massive heaps of rubble and tangled polythene. Here and there white sludge has been poured over the side of the valley, along with general builder's waste. The sludge coats once elegant terraces or fills up an otherwise empty stream bed below and is identifiable on Google Earth. The wadi is being sacrificed to development exploding from the ridge, along and down it in various forms and stages of completion. Massed flat-pack apartments will, if precedent on the south and west of the city are reliable, soon cover the steep wadi walls and fill the bottom of it too. The rubble will be invested in a road and an imported modernity will roll on towards Ain Qiniya. Soon some foreign-educated *ingénue* will suggest bridging the wadi with an inhabitable Bridge of Peace and Ramallah will be complete.

Yet I'm arguing with myself in defence of this thoughtless developmental grab. It signifies many things, central to which is a shift in parts of the Palestinian mindset. Responding to these physical facts as a human being, my heart sinks, lifts, sinks again. How to write this? How to find the words?

Occupation following ethnic cleansing combined with permanent assault has forged a form of stasis—a denial of times past and suspension of any future—which Palestinians have also partially embraced as a form of resistance. This permanent temporariness has been preserved by the world since 1948, but life is not possible in chronic stasis, if only because it's always slipping backwards. These newly confident if compromised and compromising developments, this investment in Ramallah itself, represents a shift. In part, it signals new confidence in creating or rehearsing some form of Palestinian state. This is what the building rising all around me in the wadi expresses.

Now Palestinians are changing the facts on the ground, except, of course, this is what its enemies want and encourage. Yet honesty insists that change creates momentum and that both are unpredictable.

Beyond the sludge is my first pool of Palestinian water. It marks a point at which the natural beauty of the place is reasserting itself, the peculiar enveloping 'silence' now muffles the distant rat a tat tat of construction drilling. So much so that I hear a frog grumping, which reconjures the conservationist vision that Raja Shehadeh, who lives above and further along the wadi himself, has so successfully articulated. His cleverly romanticised vision of this place has succeeded in getting the English-speaking world to notice and buy into a seductive mythology built around the location of his family's stone shelter or *qasr* on their agricultural terraces. Beyond is the reality of a wadi on or within the limits of the city, which is something else.

I enter a widening flood plain where Bedouins have built makeshift shelters in a paddock of olive trees interspersed with animal enclosures. Voices trill from within and ahead I can see a van parked up, people sitting in the mottled light opposite. Up above me on the right side is the last of Surda's new towering estates, opposite similar white walled, red roofed high-rises on the Ramallah side which look quite grand in the diminishing light. Ahead is more of the same capping a great low hill of coloured strata dotted with olive bushes and trees. A sandy line of foundational ambition cuts around the hill's belly.

Despite it all, the valley is full of peaceful airs and as I reach the people sitting roadside, they invite me to join them. I sit with the visiting van owner and two men wearing constrictively angular dress, hats, moustaches and unusual expressions. One has a slender silver tea pot, three glasses stacked on its spout and offers me some of what they've been drinking in the glowering sun. After a couple of shots of very sweet minty tea I make my apologies and keep on, determined to reach Ain Qiniya before sun fall.

Beyond the valley Ramallah proper looms high-up between the hills like a medieval lure. One hill further on and the view opens on a major tributary linking back into the heart of the city just below al Manara downtown and beginning to suffer with the overspill. The flanks of the wadi I'm trailing are far more starkly seductive; barely vegetated but roundly attractive and possessing a fierce aridity of burnt reds, white stones, dark green olive bushes, topped at this moment, by a fantastically blue sky. A fuller view of the same opens around the next hill which is also where the rubble runs out and the wadi starts to come alive.

Hills interlock before me so that I cannot see my way ahead and now the road performs a dramatic squiggle of its own to work back to the bottom of the wadi again. I can hear the bark of a human voice and distant melody of animal bells heading my way. By the time I reach the bottom, a large herd of goats has made its way up, along the road and is setting off up the track in the other wadi. Looking back after them, I'm surprised again by how Ramallah's business-like face looks like an El Dorado at this remove, at this time of day, from this wadi, in this light.

I nurse my way happily along the wadi, while al Tireh itself looms into view very high above me. The whole face of the valley is terraced and treed and at the bottom on the opposite bank of the deeply cut stream from the road is a well preserved qasr. Below that are some pools of water in the rocky-bottomed wadi and for the first time I think I'm seeing the place as it was, as other wadis further out must still be.

In a few days, I'll be crossing this wadi with friends, having climbed down terraces 200 metres high above. It takes much longer than that suggests zigzagging down to Ain al-Qasr—near the Roman-dressed spring—from the end of Salah'ddin Street above. When we do, A and L interrupt sweetly voiced songs of liberation at the sight of a mass of tall dry thistles; "the soldiers are protecting the qasr!"—a word that also means castle, even palace. We keep on along the dry river bottom, searching out the small rounded stones for the taboon, on over ridges far to the north and down into remote wadis, sleeping under trees, waking to the sight of a Palestinian sun bird; "nobody can catch him, *yanni*".

Around the next corner the wadi opens out on a major development high up on the hill. All the elements already in play gather in a single image; hand made stone terraces, ruined and well restored qasrs, gorgeous flanks of hill and established terraces carved into by fierce banks of infrastructural development, great walls of white apartment blocks—just like those in the larger settlements all around. It represents the most testing feature of this propositional Palestine. If it's indistinguishable from the work of the Occupation, with its illiterate disinterest in the place and abstract construction of space, then is it Palestinian at all?

When I first saw these developments from George Habash Square I couldn't tell whether they were new settlements or not. They resemble them closely, sometimes use the same designers, engineers, methods, perhaps even builders—just as the much-trumpeted new city of Rawabi near Nablus will do. While not settlements as such, they're developments sanctioned by the Occupation and International allies who want Ramallah to be the future capital of Palestine. At the same time homes are being bulldozed in Jerusalem, '48 Palestinians are forbidden to build, thousands have citizenship revoked each year and settlements expand all over Occupied Palestine. So does it matter? Does anything matter?

Once I put the hill and its blocked-up valley behind me again, I enter a stretch of the wadi that is entirely blissful. This is really the real wadi, one that has been here for generations, centuries. The terracing is mature and alive, the olive trees it supports are deep green and silvery leafed in the sun, qasrs dot each side and the quiet is now dominated by birdsong. Up ahead, where the steep hill is dark in shadow, sunlight flickers over mature olive trees in another wider section and a customised BMW—of all things—is parked up under the trees.

Mahmoud and two friends are chilling in the mottled shade of a golden evening. The bonnet of the car has become a bar and they're finishing a large bottle of *arak*. Ramallah is reputed to produce the strongest and having welcomed me quickly to their country I soon feel its 'kick'. Mahmoud refills a tall glass generously, talks a bit about the village north of Birzeit where they've driven down from to sit here in the peace. I decline a lift more than once and they seem to appreciate why I'm doing what I am doing—though the sun has lowered now. Quietly, Mahmoud tells me that where we are is a bit dangerous, that I should be careful, that they know to be careful themselves here. Nearby are settlers, who can do anything; "you know this?" I do, though I know less than I think I do about where we actually are. Mahmoud assures me in his well tempered voice that "we are not afraid of them. No. No Palestinian is afraid of them." His voice, its volume and tone betrays a sweetness of character that is very Palestinian in my experience. "We want to live our lives, do what we want, *yanni*."

I weigh the extravagance of such a thought here. Of course in a way they are doing what they want; taking possession of this

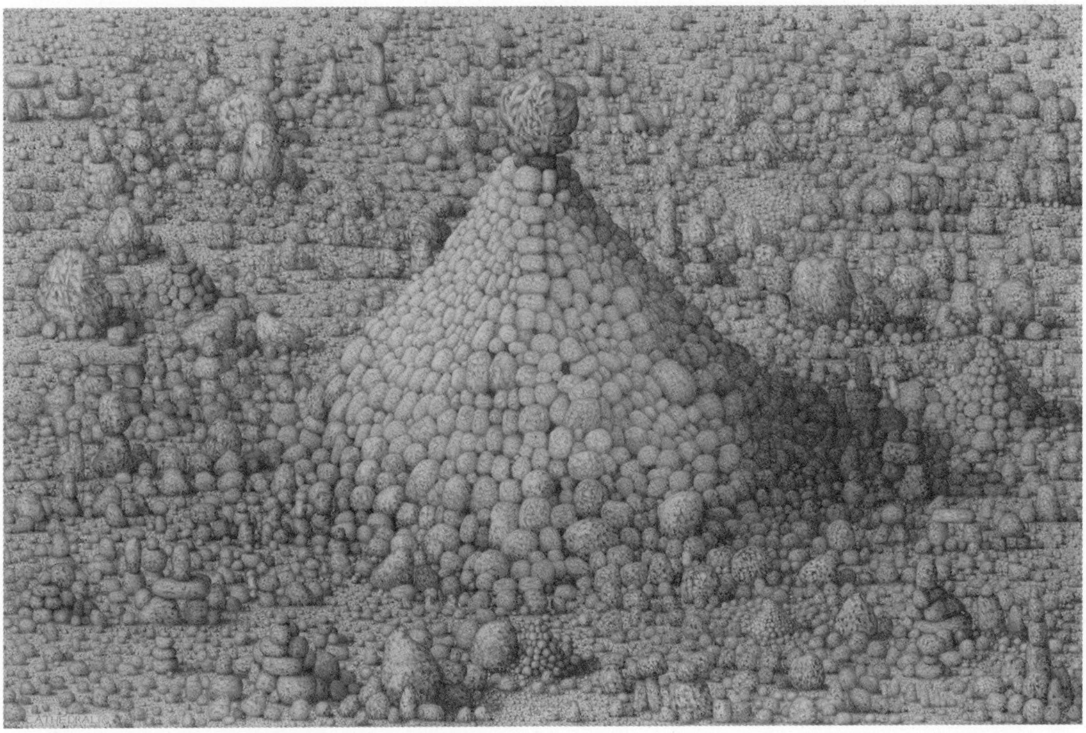

blissful hour and place—except that it's transgressive. If caught here by settlers or soldiers they are immediately outlaws, the consequences unpredictable but potentially very serious. It's not the same thing as doing what you want, is it?

Days later I'll return this way with A and L. We head north up the qasr-clad wadi behind where Mahmoud had parked his BMW, through a half-built residential estate, down into valleys and over ridges as far north as Jibiya. We will be doing what we want, certainly unafraid, singing and laughing. At the same time A—like most of the refugees at al Jalazon—cannot return to his ancestral village outside Yaffa. Life like this is possible, but only just.

I'm the only one doing exactly what I want as I continue along an increasingly golden valley, supreme relaxedness doubled by light-headedness. The road rises and descends as the valley opens out again into something of glory. A great gentle curl of a valley expands on the right of the road with terraces and qasrs quilting the entire expanse. On one craggy corner of the hill before me a ruined qasr channels glimmering sunlight out over the valley. It is a radiant sight; the fecundity of this valley and sheer proliferation of working qasrs I can see; seven or eight with my naked eye immediately, more as I pass through 360 assertive degrees. There is birdsong, a significant colour spectrum of plant life and silvery light, a perfect sanctuary of hills all around.

A sign for Ramallah on the inclining road ahead signals unintentionally that the craggily qasr'd hill is the one below George Habash Square, with a gash in its side and a stripped-back area on the top. Ain Qiniya is on its far side, reached from here by road or the wadi laid open to the right and north of the hill. I've long wondered what it would be like to stand here and yet could not imagine how stunning it would be to my senses. So engaging and relaxing is it that I forget what I do know about where I am, within the limits. I turn and savour it again; a film-poem of all that is so elementally Palestinian, how it feels to be here, how it is in this place.

I hadn't noticed the big yellow sign that I can now see advertising Dangerous Curves to drivers heading towards Surda, and still miss the significance of its repetition in Hebrew and then, in very small writing, Arabic. I turn to obey the sign to Ramallah, saving Ain Qiniya for another day, or rather for daylight, and start climbing up instead. Within 500 metres I've been asked by three creaking village cars whether I need a lift up; two of which just pulled up next to me opening the door. I explain to the sweet bemusement of each driver that I want to walk. Then the last or first house in Ramallah looms; a film set of a bunker-like creation, with a stark balcony built out over the road high up on the top floor. F calls down from it with an offer of coffee. An offer that has expanded by the time he's unchaining the big metal gates further up the road and welcoming me in.

Inside the place feels flood derelict; dark and scattered with discarded objects. F and W live here during the week, work together in Ramallah's industrial zone, head north and south of the city at weekends. Utilities don't extend this far down the wadi, so they live without electricity, rely on F's laptop to charge at work so that they can watch the occasional film or even some of the ongoing World Cup—or *Mondial.* F's offer was that in exchange for coffee we would sit savouring the sun setting from the balcony and have a proper conversation. Then in the decisive darkness he, or in fact F's older junior house mate and colleague W, will drive me back up to town, no ifs or buts.

We sit watching the view grow increasingly stunning as the light fades. First, two men drive to the bottom of the hill below, move aside the rubble blocking the road and drive up the gash in the side to the top, where F tells me people flock on Thursday nights to picnic, chill out. Now that the Occupation watch tower has been removed from the hill, that is. Later a young artist describes just such an evening spent there. By then I've been reminded of the way that road blocks and checkpoints detailed the top and bottom of this road and the east and west of the wadi along route 463, a road that was built for the settlement of Dolev nearby. That the whole wadi was a "closed area" until recently, settlers and solders would shoot at anyone seen in it; walkers, fruit pickers, that it's Area C—even if that is quite ambiguous on the ground, as I've just experienced.

Mainly, I sit and am enlightened by the power of electricity and the view it allows me here. Nearby the settlement of Dolev is brightly lit from within the forested hill directly ahead, various buildings made peculiarly distinct in flooding light. Far down below in the wadi are the occasional, insistent sparkles of Ain Qiniya; the colour if not the product of firelight. High up to the right of it on the ridge is the settler outpost of Talmon asserting itself by all means possible.

Far beyond both in distance and clarity of statement are the glowing plains of old Palestine at the bottom of the hills 15 to 20 kilometres away. Down there is a sea of light. It shimmers with constant activity and is immovably massive at the same time; a sea of power. Its signals are mortifying from up here because it's out of bounds, off limits, despite or because of being the home of so many refugees stranded in these imprisoned hills. For me it's startling, disturbing and so vulgar in its celebration of might that it's very hard to look while I'm also mesmerised by it too. I cannot imagine how much of a taunt this would be, is, every single night of the life of any Palestinian who can bear to look.

W drives me back up and in to town at a madly excited pace and I pretend I live a lot closer to George Habash Square than I do, honour satisfied. As I walk back up to my hilly home I hold to the sweet pleasures, beauty and mesmerising qualities of the wadi, email the good news to a new friend who replies; "you make it sound so lovely here!" It's her exclamation mark that makes me reflective overnight and I rise early to piece together exactly where I've been, haunted by visual proximity to the plains and old Yaffa. Abstract colour coding which actually defines the possibility of life here is now peculiarly concrete; real places with spatial qualities that are indelible. Now I realise what maps and other resources were signalling, what they actually meant. Quickly, the truth of the walk that I'd taken, the experiences I'd watchfully absorbed, what it had meant to me in the real time and place of it, multiply or double to become something new. A new time and new place. A new story from within and overriding the old one. A story or stories at the core of what Ramallah is. It is an experience of being within limits so abstract and layered that they multiply after the event. Limits which changed my own direct experience into something else. Limits which go on working insidiously, long after they have worked with murderous force. Limits that are arbitrary, lack meaning and justice, whose very unpredictability is their real power. Unpredictable limits which have come to define Palestinians' relationship to place, their place, and the life that is possible in or on it.

I'd started to assume that development on the far side of the wadi that seems to provide a natural limit to Ramallah was evidence of the city expanding. In fact, the northerly ridges are divided into two further municipalities; Surda and Ain Qiniya, both of which rationalise Occupation boundaries. The idyllic wadi junction where I drank arak with Mahmoud and gang was beyond the old road block to its east. Until recently the people of Ain Qiniya were beyond a further full checkpoint and the military's watch tower and yet another road block separated them from the outskirts of Ramallah above, at what is now George Habash Square. The balcony where I drank conversational coffee and saw the torturous reality of brightly illuminated dispossession is a recent result of military withdrawal.

Within the limits, all limits become abstract. Increasingly this is the story everywhere I go here, a production of this particular Occupation. It leaves people not only displaced and dispossessed, but unplaced, unpossessed. To confront limits, to breach them, you have to know what and where they are. This is why in the prison of these hills, in lovely Ramallah itself, there is no freedom. Here, in this place, life spirals within abysmal limits.

In Ramallah, I'm running within bodily limits; the muscular fruits of midnight runs along the river in Central London. Here I run from the centre to its limits, as far as I'm able. Within my limits means running for twice as long if not twice as far as in London. Ramallah is small and so am I.

I'm running within the limits of what I understand of what I can see in Ramallah. I pass Edward Sa'id Street which is easy, though repeatedly Abu Q regrets its modest scale. Down past al Raja'a (Hope) Street which is less easy but surely always involves the same deal? In any case I keep running far beyond Hope Street and back again. "Pain is inevitable, suffering is optional", the novelist points out, "whether or not you can stand anymore is up to the runner (her)self."

Running takes me places I would not otherwise go; past the end of Rachel Corrie Street, for example. It takes me along the ridge past the beginnings of Dalal Mughrabi, Nile and Nativity Streets and out to George Habash Square. On my return I concentrate on the writers who seem even more arbitrarily heralded in this way; streets named after Lorca and Louis Aragon, for example. I circle back to Edward Sa'id Street, just as I did to him and his work.

In Ramallah, nobody recognises or cares about al Jihad Street or the tarmac of George Habash Square. The game of naming is the oldest colonial trick, paid for this time by USAID. Yet seeing the names going up intrigues me in ways that seeing traditional stone houses or refugee apartments take on a number does not. Stories of love or hate attach to names in ways that they don't to the number 21 or 118.[1] Everyone here blames Occupation and official Palestinian weakness for the cancelled memorialising of Dalal Mughrabi Square. The same, apparently, happened with George Habash Square. Perhaps I've "seen the name on a map".

I stop running at Lorca Street halfway up a long hill where the road bends beyond sight of friendly guards outside the Chinese Embassy. I can't help laughing out loud when I realise what I've done again. While Dalal Mughrabi was too controversial for a square to be named after her, the signpost I run past seems overlooked or unseen. As I approach Rachel Corrie Street I think of older 'sisters' met here who are finding ways to turn protest into substantive commitment. Near the bottom of the road named for her a big Caterpillar digger is at work, making for complications. It is me that is running.

Walking or climbing the final steep stretch home, habit etching residence in these hills, I understand better an elliptical phrase of the novelist's. Long term projects, he wrote, involve both concentrated focus and endurance. They involve "continuing to breathe while holding your breath". Impossible seeming, it might be a potent enough paradox for how Ramallah is—at least for now.

Within the Without.

I dedicated my first full day in Ramallah to memorials. It took a lifetime to get here; I wanted to honour some of the things that brought me and then leave them behind, at least for now. So I went to make a wish for the compromised Yasser Arafat at his mausoleum or *maqbara* on the outskirts of the city, the old colonial Muqata where the world watched Occupation tanks almost kill him. Abu Ammar, or more cannily Abu Muhammad as he was once known, is buried in a peculiarly affecting Minimalist complex, designed to be transported to his final resting place in Jerusalem. Outside is a plaque on the wall marking how close and yet far it remains; 16.43 kilometres.

I went to pay more clarified respects to Mahmoud Darwish, using the route his funeral cortege took from the Muqata to the hill top on the south-west of the city, above Rafat. It's also a temporary home, not because the National poet of Palestine is likely to be moved (though he had no love of Ramallah), but because a memorial museum and archive will be built on the hill, designed by the same architect. It will be named al Birwa Park after the village of his birth in old Palestine which was emptied out and then erased. A weighty gravestone bears characteristic lines which translate as "in/on this earth there is something to live for".

I spent some of my Memorials Day with Mourid Barghouti's new memoir, *I Was Born There, I Was Born Here*—though happily he's vigorously alive and writing poems in Cairo. However, his first memoir told of returning to Ramallah and his home village of Deir Ghassanah after 30 years in exile. It's a classic which I know intimately well from having been asked to write the introduction to Mourid's first selection of poetry in English. I wanted to cherish a privileged intimacy and then have Ramallah to myself; it is me that is running.

I found Mourid's books at the same place I found a copy of Ghassan Kanafani's *Men in the Sun*, one of few titles I recognise in Arabic; *Rijal fii al Shams*. I walked down to the late opening bookstore nearby on my very first evening and, faced with an overwhelming ocean of Arabic, held to what I knew. Amongst the fat handful of Kanafani's slim books, all of them printed in Nicosia, Northern Cyprus, I couldn't resist a copy of *Rijal fii al Shams* in Arabic.

On the way back up through the hospitals that almost block off Hospital Road, I bought my first Palestinian falafel in a small empty café near the corner of what turned out to be Ghassan Kanafani Street. I didn't know the name of the street that first evening, of course. When I did find it on the map, I returned and used it as a short cut to al Bireh one day, passing through Qaddura refugee camp. I didn't know it was Qaddura refugee camp that day either, for reasons that are more complicated than familiarity with a map or this city.

Al Amari Refugee camp is the largest camp in Ramallah itself, founded in '48 on the outskirts of the town beyond al Sharafa, the old farewell point on the road to Jerusalem. Tents were pitched on land in villages all around Ramallah and like those camps al Amari has grown into a complex warren of tightly jammed homes, temporary in spirit and appearance. The United Nations leased land from owners on 99 year leases and to this day maintains elementary food supplies and some responsibility for those it officially recognised. The abysmal temporariness of life in these camps is an accurate symbol of the neglect the world has shown to Palestinians for over six decades. The fact that the leases are nearing term is grotesque.

The camps are home to the most committed resistance to Occupation, the people stuck in them having most to fight for and nothing else to lose. Amongst many shared characteristics there are subtle differences too. Al Jalazon camp to the north of the city shares visual qualities with al Amari and others; concrete shuttered improvisations, hopeless infrastructural jams, posters of Abu Jihad and other *shahids*; fighters, bystanders, farmers and students. However, this was known as the Green Camp and is populated by people forced out of villages around Yaffa on the plains below. Sitting in its midst with friends one evening I couldn't help notice how it retains the atmospheric manners of a village, despite being the size of a town nowadays, any greenery beyond its limits.

Qaddura is different altogether, always controversial because *Nakba*-survivors found an apparently empty quarter even then close to the modern centre of the city and took refuge in houses left empty by migrants to the United States, erecting tents in-between. The UN has never recognised it officially, so it has never 'benefited' from UNHCR relief programmes, though there's a PLO Refugee Committee presence (Jerusalem 14 kilometres). The camp itself now takes the form of two and a bit blocks of dense urban tenements filling a strip of land that descends into a built-up wadi so that there are no views out east or west. It is situated between Ramallah and al Bireh, in the middle of the joint city—within limits, yet still without.

In 2002 it was attacked with tanks and artillery, on one occasion a journalist was killed and many others wounded. More recently it has been subject to raids by the same Occupation army, men arrested at night, sometimes killed, incursions with no end. On the city map published in 2003, it's marked out very clearly between streets named after Kanafani and Abd al-Qader al-Husseini. On the 2010 map of new Ramallah, it no longer exists.

I'd walked past it unwittingly a couple of times as I got to grips with Ramallah, one morning I walked to it instead. Where the main road cuts through its western extremity the relative impoverishment of the place is visible to me now. The sheer walled buildings are poorly maintained, very nearly the only walls in the city that carry shahid posters and graffiti nowadays. High up on one side images of Abu Ammar and Sheikh Yassin and then Marwan Barghouti have all faded back to the colour of the dirty wall into which they have been painted over and are slowly merging.

On one corner there is an easily-missed diagonal entrance to the interior of the block. I slip into its high narrow embrace and enter a different world, a highly interior one of shadows and narrow corridors, turning abruptly, no sight lines. All I can see are the varying forced staircases ascending wherever they can, entrances high up, incoherent. I keep going, an obvious intruder in what is still public space, but not wanting to frighten anyone. There's no-one here in the 'street', though voices emerge from discretely raised windows. Buildings seem to merge into an interconnected tenement block which is home to hundreds of people, yet the word labyrinthine which it owns seems too big for it.

My sense of vulnerability is proportionate to the shock I'll give anyone who meets me, so it's quite high. Door, windows, external landings angle above, then a dark alley jags back, my own runs out of light and I turn and see another, hanging down almost blocking it is a new banner commemorating the killing of someone in November 2009. As I walk back the way I came, a young girl hears my footsteps and skips after me, only to reveal confused horror when we meet at the exit. In contrast to the confidently engaging boys and girls—rich and poor—met across the city and far beyond, she is unable to get over her shock enough to reply to my greetings.

I walk around the outside of the same block, down the slope to where a road—named after a river in Syria—divides the camp in two. From the outside, especially where it seems as if there are ways in through illegible building mass, rusty corrugated steel and refuse, it looks much more wretched than the orderly albeit breathless interior it contains. I turn and notice a tidied up derelict site, begin to realise that improvised stencilling on the far wall means it is a play area for camp children. At that moment two boys appear and confirm my impression with happy excitement. This is the nearest they have to public space, but the thought highlights a wider predicament. Public in what sense? What is the collectivity here? Who speaks or acts for it? As private space a plot like this is very valuable; a cleared one on the edge of the camp neighbours a bar where the talk is of one or two million dollars.

When I turn to photograph the exterior of the main residential blocks, excitement turns to anxiety and prohibition. No, no I must not photograph here, no photographs of the camp, no no. On the main road a trolley vendor had said the same thing when I turned to take a general photograph of Hospital Road. He was very insistent, no photographs and definitely no photographs with him in them, not that he was ever in frame. He kept repeating his injunction inanely, an old woman shuffled by tutting and I wondered about it.

The camp has a peculiar intimacy; when I pass at other times of day I see his trolley left unmanned, with an indicative sheet over his goods. Now these boys are showing how early threats to life are imbibed here, how often they must've heard related injunctions, how preyed upon they are. I hear the same sharp defensiveness in other places of maximum vulnerability, or from people who have already experienced the arbitrary terrors of Occupation in short or long detentions without charge or trial. Or whose family or friend has become a shahid.

My own wrongness is not the point here except for the fear that any such photograph or information about access to the interior of the camp gets into the wrong hands. The wrong hands are possessed by those who come at night in APCs with exotic military capability to snatch anyone from their bed that they wish. So often these raids end in the death of so-called "militants" who "resist". Raids are not imaginary but constant, taking place throughout (before, during and after) my short residence here, though Ramallah itself enjoyed a short period of relief.

Photographs of Qaddura show what a refugee camp that is not a refugee camp in the middle of Ramallah looks like. How different it is from its context, the overt poverty, the absence of a single stone villa or person very nearly. Most dramatically the way in which the inside is hidden from the street, within a protective shell, coiled up bearing protective needles. It is a world of its own, within itself. It is within the without; an intrusive organ within the host body which is itself under mortal threat.

I'm reminded of a note of the poet's in a scrupulously exact and honest memoir. "We too have our faults, our share of short-sightedness", he writes. "How can we explain today... that we on the West Bank treated our people as refugees.... We called them immigrants!" It's a general remark and he does not elaborate, but I thought of these words while standing inside Qaddura. There's a tension between people here and those around, few continuities between camp interior and the city outside. Except, that is, resemblance to the old city around the main mosque, where worn stone buildings crowd each other, displaying improvisation, labyrinthine access and a marked interiority. I met with some wariness on the first couple of explorations and the same old prohibition when I returned for a third time to photograph the architecture of the back streets.

Ramallah was founded by Greek Orthodox Christians and remained Christian past the point that it became a city a century ago. After 1948 that changed as a direct result of the great influx of refugees from the plains below. Ramallah became a majority Muslim city for the first time and presumably most of those refugees—the poet's self-critical "immigrants"—arrived with nothing. The architectural sensibility of the old town and Qaddura is Islamic, whatever the contingencies of the latter's coming-into-being. Those bent entrances, narrow corridors, high windows, general emphatic interiority are classic features of many traditional Muslim communities. Here they are as distinct as is an insecurity about status shared with the people I met in the old town. Insecurity that I did not find in Nablus for example, where most of these elements are fully embodied in the old walled city. Where I was invited up and on to roofs to photograph the interior courtyards and domed quarters of their resilient city.

Qaddura is a zone without limits; inside and yet without the limits of the city. It reminds me of the philosopher's thoughts on receiving new life in the form of a heart transplant. "This gaping cannot be sealed up", he wrote, "I am closed open." The arrival of the intrusive organ is a gift which "institutes the possibility of a network" an opening out to the other in "on-growing infinity". His body is now a zone without limits; the new heart is inside and yet definitely without the limits of its body. Yet; "the intruder is nothing but myself and man himself. None other than the same...."

In these ways Qaddura is the least and most representative place in Ramallah; within the limits, without. When I next pass through it there are new shahid posters on the wall signed with the PFLP's 'return' logo—pasted up under a new number 41. When we identify who they honour, Issa's friends describe his fierce intelligence and committedness, how he was shot in the head at a demonstration in the city; deliberately targeted. His death, stirred by my talk of memorial posters, is a closed open wound.

Running in Ramallah was tough today, I don't know why.

Usually running melts problems down but it didn't today. Sundays are busy here; traffic roared right to the last connected suburb along al Tireh—which means almost to the end. In any break, the security guys zoomed about, shifting positions with puzzling urgency. Running back, construction drilling kicked up across the wadi, a noise that the nervous would ascribe to artillery. This morning I sympathise, but have spied on the only shooting I've heard here. From a rubble-strewn road below Ramallah's sewage works, an artillery range within the Occupation's military base can be looked down upon. Yet there is deadliness in this drilling too.

Running in Ramallah was effortsome, like everything else at the moment. Am I finding Ramallah hard and therefore the running or is it the other way round? The days are suddenly hotter, I'm dry throated, coughing as if ill and truly stiffened. Last night I stepped out into the wet nudges of a cloud on my homely hill, thought to myself stupidly; "it's raining too!" This morning, running was physically hard; every incline felt like two, each slope shouted at me to stop, every kilometre contained a thousand metres. Two days ago, identical conditions set me alight, drowned me in my own happy sweat and felt like a breeze.

In Ramallah, not running is tough. I'm not tired of the place but am finding it hard going, feeling every small difficulty, noticing every easing off or upward struggle with scepticism. I've completed some laps now and it's getting harder to avoid the disabling virus of NGOisation which flourishes in conditions like these. Even a best friend emails to ask if I'm hating it here yet. The only way to be completely free of what they mean is to rely on my own physical and intellectual resources and their limits. What that means is wearying to contemplate.

Running back and about to turn off Yaffa Street, a pretty tune strikes up within—unburdened with words and then suddenly not. "I found a little plot of land, in the garden of Eden / It was dirt and dirt is all the same / I tilled it with my two hands and I called it my very own / There was no-one to dispute my claim." It's a song I saw performed in London by Joanna Newsome and her harp with such startling clarity that it lives in me exactly as it was received. Running against the grain has at least relaxed me.

In Ramallah I'll hold to my contrapuntal interior for now; it's me that is running.

At the Limits.

I'm wondering about the what, where and how of limits and then, apparently more prosaically, about the limits of Ramallah. Legal limits laid down in the mid-90s during 'Oslo' are somewhere in my head, though not in mind. Recent statements about expanding those limits and how each case is negotiated individually, too. Then I have the evidence of my eyes which contrasts with almost all of this to confusing effect. So I resort to my feet.

Early one morning I walk west on the Yaffa Road through Beitunia, assuming that something somewhere will be open for breakfast like downtown Ramallah. My route follows Beitunia's development along the road to Ain Arik which carries on west until the hills end at Bil'in with the notoriously foreshortening wall. The last of new-Beitunia's steep hill is lined with expectant building materials, beyond which I turn off it up a little lane that will twist around and down a wadi to Ain Qiniya. At the top of the lane are factory farms for chickens, otherwise nothing but super-arid terrain. If I'm going to eat this morning, I'll have to find a way up to al Mazra'a al Qibliya.

The wadi descends quickly once more, the silence deep and homely. It is still early enough to be cool, for my footsteps to wake wild dogs in panic. The big hill to the left is spartan and dry in the way I like and rounds spectacularly. Above it, though not visible once in the wadi, is a communication mast which towers over Ain Arik far below on its west side. Ahead of me, down the deepening wadi, is the pleasing dark green of fig and olive groves, the varying shades of fruit trees and giant cacti. Lastly, I can see Ain Qiniya's elegant white mas'jid from quite a distance, amongst a scattering of dark grey walled square dwellings.

This is Ramallah at the limits—within the outside, that threshold of the oldest of cities—where livestock is kept to supply kitchens within. Westwards are four delimiting hills; the southern is an enclosed military zone, the north overlooks Ain Qiniya which used to mark the limits with massed checkpoints. As I descend towards it a range of settlements stand to attention. To the west is Dolev, almost hidden in trees, east of which is a bare rocky hill topped with a military watch tower above the village below. Beyond and straight ahead are two faces of Talmon; an outpost with communication masts and white caravans atop a very high hill and to its west the standard cluster of red-topped 'burbs, all towering over the wadis that Ain Qiniya nestle in.

I keep going down this blissful vale, passing tall pink hollyhocks waving in the breeze, until red-ripe plums loom invitingly from unusually healthy trees beside the road. With my hunger unshakeable, I remember something I'm often told; "it is your right, *yanni*, to take as you want; not more. You can take, it is your *right*, but not, *yanni*, not fill your pockets! Just you eat there, in the place—as you want." If anyone were standing here I know he or she would insist I took a handful too, but taking them myself is different. It is not an agonising call and I appreciate the ironies. It's a beautiful notion as a right, but pretentious to claim it as mine.

Ain Qiniya is a pretty and well farmed valley which becomes clearer the closer I get to it. *Ain* means spring, of course, and at the bottom of the wadi are the greenest looking trees I've seen anywhere in the District. The closer I get the more the Occupation looms too, signalling presence, control and the power of surveillance. They might be watching me now as I watch them, indeed that is my presumption. I'm more intrigued by how basic the village dwellings are; square, grey-rendered, with small high windows, no signs of life and yet as I pass nearby, gay female voices pour out from within. At the river bed, empty but for a small pool, the valley muscles westwards beyond Dolev, access reputedly 'blocked' by the new settler road that replaced route 463 towards Surda. I stand before a steeply banked slope to the south, all neatly terraced with farmhouses high up on the side. Following the ridge westwards, I think it must be Deir Ibzi that I can see mustered in white, but it could be Kafr Nima; perspective abandons you once buried in this embracing landscape.

Up on the main road, two men sit waiting for an early morning servee. Unusually both ignore my greetings and attempts to discover how to get to al Mazra'a. Eventually the older of the two, who had militantly closed his eyes, points me in the right direction towards the mas'jid now out of sight. Meanwhile, I've noticed something smoking under roadside trees further beyond them. Walking towards it I find a woman and her daughter working away at a traditional taboon 'oven'. Unresponsive male relatives sit around the little yard, but the younger woman and I exchange greetings. Both women are flush-faced with their work and the heat of the fire, seem further flustered as well as pleased by my attention.

In downtown Ramallah, taboons are churned out of a machine directly onto the pavement for a shekel. Big, thick, heavy breads, they retain their classic scooped or bubbled appearance by way of lumps on the metal rollers. Here is the real thing; an iron drum containing a floor of rounded stones heated from below, upon which lie four baking breads. These stones are smaller than the metal lumps, but bigger than those A and I selected from the nearby wadi's bottom for use on a hearth at al Jalazon.

As we exchange elementals, the older woman looks at me worriedly, then happily even eagerly reaches for the best done taboon, lifts it off gently and hands it to me; hot, floppy and delicious-looking. She refuses to let me pay for it; calmly giving me what she can, realising that I'll enjoy it, guessing that I need it. My mind scrambles as I recall the poet telling me that people in the villages will do this; give you anything that they have, just like this. Now it's more important to receive her gift properly, I think, so don't disguise my pleasure. This evident appreciation registers in half smiles on the faces of both women and definite glints of pleasure in their eyes. Parting, I bite into it heartily, very nearly wink at the two now-smiling men along the road and am welcomed to the village by the newly arrived servee driver. Now I have every possible means and opportunity to climb up to al Mazra'a, if only I can find the way.

Through the village and beyond the mas'jid the valley starts to open, groves of well cared-for trees spill each side as I commit to one of two good tracks aiming for the wadi between two big hills ahead. Through the trees on my left I can see the watch tower, but still feel no anxiety about it today. The further along the track I go the more beautiful the valley becomes and the more beckoning the quiet. Then as a restored stone building appears up ahead, the sound of running water leaps into the amplifying valley. To my right now is the wadi that links around the hill into the glorious qasr-filled zone that I admired from the road from Surda just before turning up towards George Habash Square. On my left there is a blue shirted Bedouin herding goats in the distance down in the wet part of the wadi. Ahead is a ford over the noisily happy stream. Very far up above us are the scars of settlements with their treasured vantage points, symbolic security and condescension, their stupid inability to appreciate that eternal life resides down here.

The moment I hit the steep pathway that cuts through trees—large free-standing rocks and cacti up ahead, shed snake skins below—crickets explode into a great storm of alarm which drops away as I keep climbing. The path is a good one, obviously relied upon by people coming or going some distance regularly. I stop and turn to look back at Ain Qiniya and see that it has been absorbed into an extremely pretty view.

Turning back and digging in for the climb I spot a beer bottle covered in Hebrew on the path ahead. It's a warning sign, a reminder of what I know of where I am. Directly above the path ahead is the settler outpost of militants with their white caravans. High up on the other side and slightly further away are the skeletal forms of new developments which I know now must be Palestinian and which are linked by a track or road back several kilometres towards Birzeit. It's the middle of three ridges in fact, the first directly links to Abu Qash, while the third is the ridge that al Mazra'a is spread along.

I've never figured out how to get to al Mazra'a's ridge from here. My only resource shows the steep path expiring then a gap before a farm of some kind sits in the valley beyond which seems to be a road. I do not know how these elements link up, whether that will get me to al Mazra'a or whether the path and farm are 'owned' by the settlers who now look much closer to it than I could determine remotely. The beer bottle is unequivocal but I'm not going to stop now. I've got a steep hill to climb, a path to find, a village to visit, authoritative views to gain, limits to clarify.

Speaking of clarifying perspective, it's only now that I realise my appearance in Ain Qiniya would resemble that of the settler's beer bottle. The guardedness it generated the same as that of the owner of a supermarket near my home on the hill replying to my Arabic with Hebrew. The offence I took at this test was forgotten as an addiction grew for their strawberry juice. I probably most resembled the beer bottle when grilled one night at al Jalazon; Imperialism, Marx, God, etc. The sign-that-I-am is properly equivocal though; these small 'tests' coexist with real surprise at evidence of my watching, reading, *noticing* 'life' in Palestine over the years. This is not a place that can afford presumptions.

Ain Qiniya keeps running away with every backward and downwards glance, like a broken zoom. Soon I can see the top of hills I've climbed and suddenly there is al Tireh looming beyond the small round hill that bore the watch tower below, darkly beckoning me with its familiarity. I'm still at the limits in the shadows of coming development, not yet at the bleak portal of the settler world. Already from here the view of Palestine's hills; bare, dry, but dotted with knots of vegetation in characteristic ways, is grand and demonstrates that the gentleness and accommodating manner of the people and place are moored in each other.

When I turn back again the path has disappeared, so I finish the last crust of still-moist taboon to concentrate on the way ahead. To get beyond the walled farmland which now fills the wadi, I'm forced to cross towards the settler mast right above me. Rough hillside rises above an oasis of fig, olive and fruit trees, a kitchen garden complete with poly-tunnel full of tomatoes and zucchini, fields ahead of stubby green plants, perhaps thyme, and a rich red strip of newly tilled soil. In the midst of the latter are men bent in industry. We see each other at the same time; an awkward

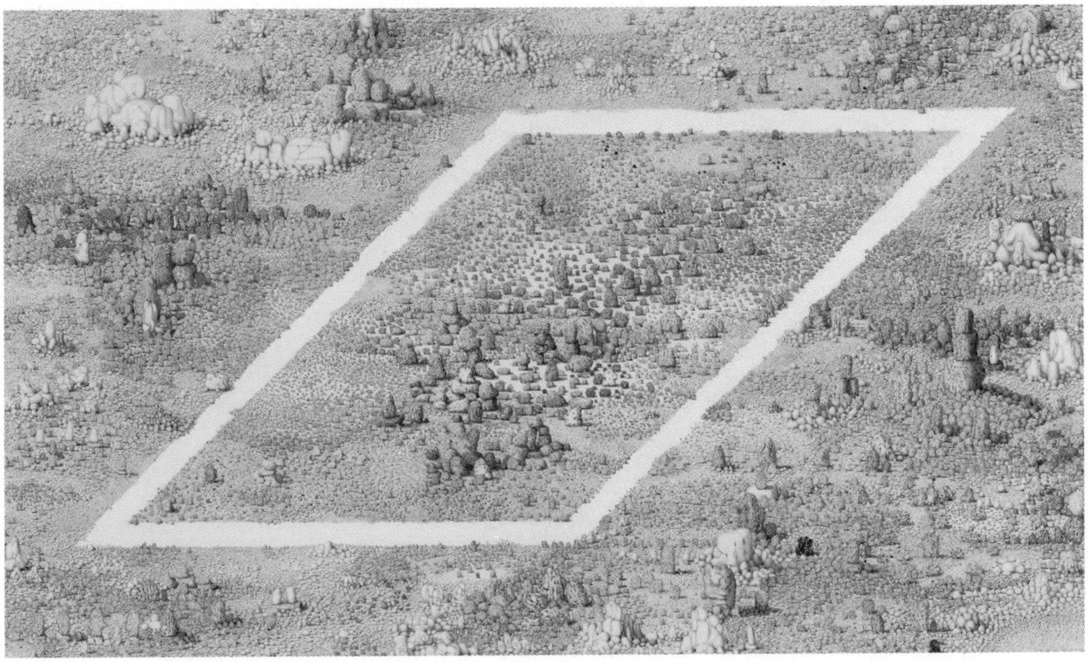

few moments. I have no idea whether they are settlers or human beings; but they're darkly silhouetted and distant enough to require that I shout out to them. I know the odds but bank on Arabic and when they reply similarly we exchange relieved greetings.

Above the farm and beyond the settler's outpost, I stop in the shade of an unusually large olive tree to savour what is now a stunning view of the hills of Ramallah. This is why I've come, this is what I'm doing here. This ties together the walking, wadis, even the running I've been doing. All the views I've had of Ramallah and its limits, north and west even south are now present and legible to me. Straight ahead is the wadi of untouched plums I descended from Beitunia, the hills with their communication masts above it. Ramallah itself floats above all the hill tops in-between us, including the golden flanks of bare concrete on the ridge linking back to Abu Qash. What I can see in all this detail and contextualising sweep makes sense of Ramallah and the interior life of the city for me.

Then there's a special gift: for the first time I can see a clear declination of the hills towards the west where they meet the plains. Only now under the tree do I realise that Bil'in—the last village in the west before the wall—must be very close to the sea level of the plains. It is clear now that to understand Ramallah's place in these hills, I need to follow them down below sea-level to Ariha/Jericho in the lunar east and continue exploring villages and hills in the west. Specifically; to follow them down to Bil'in, site of famous weekly protests at the blatantly intrusive Occupation wall. I will go and stand in that famous site of resistance because I need to see what happens as Ramallah's hilly hinterland runs out and forms a meaningful limit of its own.

All the vital life discovered in these hills also diminishes in the scale of their sweep west. The distance is small and made more so by the similar distance between its natural expiration on the plains and the forbidden sea just beyond. Only last night I climbed onto the roof of the big old house neighbouring mine on the hill and looked hard and steadily at this westerly view measured in nocturnal light. It was sickening to see what it means, the distances involved, the tininess of what is left of Palestine. Sickeningly clear that there is no more viability to the two-state compromise offered by Abu Ammar in 1988. Yet, in daylight under the big tree the defeat of being imprisoned in these small hills seems like a partial victory, because they're so defiantly lovely and full of the actual fruits of the place.

It's an easy walk from the tree to the pass which opens onto another system of wadis, hills, Palestinian villages and yet more settlements on hills for as far as you want to look. This is also the beginning of the end of al Mazra'a al Qibliya which stretches along the road that curls eastwards along the ridge. I walk uncertainly, ask two slow-moving women for directions before stepping into a store and astonishing its soberly civil owner. I rehydrate while we chat in Arabic and English, Abu S expressing surprise that I have walked here, turned up so early from Ramallah, Beitunia! Now the women arrive and step over to share their titillated surprise at my presence while kids run in and out. The news is shared in animated voices and the women stand looking at me less like a stumbling fool than a returning neighbour. After arming me with directions to a servee along the road, Abu S summarises with a flourish; "You are a very strong man!"

I walk on through the village to the bus stand from where distant Kobar, a hill village close to Jibiya, is enticingly visible to the north. When the servee fires up, it fills very quickly with all the people I've just encountered and the bracing odours of freshly gathered sage. The sage is on its way to market, carried on by women in the traditional embroidered dress, known as a *thob*. Some of the accompanying men are in traditional dress too, white headpieces fluttering in the open windows, held in place by that band of black. While there are discrete queries over my presence, I know we're one of many servees full of villagers doing the same thing all around Ramallah this morning.

I ponder my characterisation as a strong man. I know Abu S meant determined, clear—or perhaps strong-minded, that in terms of strength, these walks are modest affairs limited by heat and hydration. I can carry enough water to get me to about 11 or so in the morning after which the sun burns up at a different rate. The walking is not hard, even if some of the ease is a by-product of my running in Ramallah. It has been and still is essential to do what I'm doing here; pushing out and across the actual place, drawing my own conclusions, to connect and disconnect, realise fast and slowly as much as possible.

When I look at the maps again to see what I'd missed or misread about the way to al Mazra'a, I saw it immediately. Firstly, of course, the distance looks like nothing once returned from wadi to desk. Second, I had read as much as I possibly could from the images I had. What I'd missed was that the entirety of my walk today was within Area C; technically off limits, beyond the bounds. The 'discovery' didn't fill me with retroactive foreboding. Any encounter with settlers and the Occupation were potential for me, at least while beer bottles remain on the path and not in the hands of the trigger-happy.

No, the real lesson from this took a bit longer to dawn on me and it relates to Abu S. Gradually, his use of the word "strong" made sense. He was referring to my walking to al Mazra'a through Area C, which evidently doesn't happen often. Not many faces—foreign or otherwise—have stepped into his shop doorway from the left side on the way from Beitunia. Not for quite some years, not since the twentieth century at best and even then not since the mid-90s when 'Oslo' ceded so much to the Occupation.

At the limits, this is what the word "strong" means. I don't own it: al Mazra'a al Qibliya will see many more 'strong' visitors stepping across thresholds from the left, each one growing weaker than the last, weaker even than I.

In Ramallah, I'm running beyond my own bounds.

Running with a hard earned, slow building invincibility which is nothing but the joy of the run itself. The way my body feels; warmed throughout, muscles singing, stone in raining sweat. The capability lent me; the homeliness of that feeling, a muscular mastery of place. I just kept going, pushing beyond my limits to new heights of endurance and strength. A great feeling, can it last?

I've been puzzling past trees in the middle of narrow pathways. Fruit trees and conifers fill pavements around al Jihad Street. Along Bat'n al Hawa, holes are shuttered in new concrete for the coming trees. Mature ones fill the pavement along al Nuzha Street, named to signal a nice place for a walk. It leads downtown where traffic is lively, chaotic, jammed up but rarely aggressive. There's a rhythm to it; drivers allow for pedestrians—even runners—who steal along or across the tarmac. Space is Occupied but the use made of it is extravagant, improvised, negotiable. Underneath modernity's pavement is a place that is peculiarly Palestinian.

In Ramallah I'm eating and drinking in comradely circles. Coffee pots are ambushed, little cups, glasses relayed. Circles form around breakfast at 11; tahini tricks, zaatar omelettes, baby cucumbers and breads draw arms in and out under the vines, the poly-tunnel or olive trees below Silwad. For lunch at four in enervating Jericho, we surround a big hot pot of stuffed vine leaves, chicken and tomato sauce as it's turned onto a platter in the back-office. Hands dive, peck and revel. In al Jalazon a beautifully prepared dinner on big round platters of things finely stuffed and sumac'd is eagerly consumed by similar means.

Running in Ramallah, I'm thinking of the resistance offered by fire. The Occupation has stolen the earth and air of Palestine. Even the water has been stolen and siphoned back for two hours a day into big black plastic butts crowding every roof top in town. When he showed me a photograph of himself at the Mediterranean coast, during an illicit visit to his ancestral home, "Abu Muhammad's" face wore its open horizon again. Fire is something else. Venerated for millennia in India, sages also liken the immanence of Brahman—their unrepresentable divine spirit—to that of fire in wood.

In Ramallah I am running on fire.

On Limits.

Occupation works by generating so many limits that they float, shift, confuse and undo you. Limits are in every place and every time, including retroactively. But where they finally stand to fight they are so abrupt as to require ravagingly honest brevity.

On my first visit to the overflowing market in downtown Ramallah I returned with trophies boycotted at home where they are supplied by the Occupation. Principal amongst them were huge hearty red peppers which soon filled my borrowed fridge. By my last visit I'd realised that almost all the food here is supplied by the Occupation, the evidence all over the market in Hebrew-laden packaging. It is a sickening, almost final blow, even while a new campaign to enforce the boycott of settlement produce is launched. Imagine being forced to pay so many times for your own prison food.

On my final walk down the wadi towards Rafat I notice the same evidence of repackaged fruits of Occupation in a barn stacked with oranges and lemons—vegetables too. While this adds symbolic force to urgent calls for external boycotts, it's almost too mortifying a reality to face here—where the notion say, of a Non-Cooperation Movement is only a nasty joke. I walk on because I'm going to the limits again today, to chase them round to the west where I want to climb another of the city's delimiting hills.

This road shadows the prison walls, roads, lights and apparatus of the Ofer military base. Ofer generates livid scars in the landscape which are so extreme as to be perversely alluring; fascistic triumphs. As I tramp up and over this road it develops into a peculiar vision of dystopia. Within lies the massive municipal dump high up to my right, sending violent stenches into the sky. The road is a mess of rubble and then as the hill ends, so Ramallah's very own sewage works loom within. Outside the open-air works is a dark pool afloat with wild dogs. Ahead the road is crowded by massive movements of the ground. It's not clear whether rocky substrata is being removed or vast amounts of rubble and earth are simply being remodelled. The intention seems to be to block the view across the limits, which reveal the interior of the military base; its shooting range and interdictory apparatus.

Ramallah is showing its rear, its arse to the monster; "well if that's the way you want it, we shit on you!" So a small smile accompanies me up through this dusty purgatory and on down towards what soon emerges as the actual rectum hereabouts; the Ofer 'gate' and bridge from within the hilly encampment to the rest of occupied Palestine. As I peak the devastated hill, amplified shouting starts up and solders start jerking around the camp below. Someone or—thing is causing fantastic distress to a licensed shrieker, but I keep on for the opposite side of the metalled wadi below towards the old town of Beitunia on the hill. The hysteria has relented by the time I reach the gates, where lorries are parked up awaiting permission to deliver PA supplies to Gaza. I'm alone in the huge plaza area, eventually shouted at anyway but just keep walking.

Beyond Ofer to the south are the "Jerusalem Hills" and Jerusalem is visible from many places in Ramallah itself. The limits here make me more interested in views west and only now can I see that the road that curls around old Beitunia is actually within the base. I walk on and find my way past a chatty group of children who cheer me up the steep sun-glazed hill ahead. At the top is a pretty but part-derelict stone-built neighbourhood and a complete surprise to me. Restored, this will be a textbook "Heritage Opportunity". For now it's caught up in the Occupation's limits which only reveal their true extent when I try to scale the far side of the ridge.

On the west side, houses stop abruptly and terraces descend steeply before yet another livid gash through the land which marks an Occupation road. I can hardly believe my eyes because what this does is to sever any link between Beitunia and the hills, wadis and villages to the west. It's more stark at the base of the hill where the usual fencing snarls across little strips of fertile terrace, before the usual unnaturally neat road snakes northwards and blocks access to the hills opposite. Over there is a green lung; stretched limbs, heartfulls of refreshing views and the connective tissue of neighbouring villages.

Standing here, stuck down in this Occupation trap is peculiarly moving. It's surprised me this time. I feel authentic anger at having my movements obstructed, impulses denied, the simple desire to go somewhere so brutally and meaninglessly prohibited. It is the lack of sense, the impossibility of any answer to the most elemental question of why? that infuriates. Of course, it's a very minor inconvenience for me, but I can sense how frustrating it must be to have to live within this particular prison. I can feel the helplessness that limits like this generate, the way they play with you so willfully. I'm overwhelmed, actually, by furious contempt in ever more clarifying shades of black and white. I do not want it in my body or mind, but anything else would be dishonest and more degrading.

The only thing to do is find where the limits end and a way around them. I climb back up, wander through more of the old town and have warming conversation with various surprised residents—each of whom welcomes me to their country. A female shop-owner is especially curious but we struggle as I try to correct her conclusion that I'm half-Palestinian in Arabic. I take the compliment and follow instructions back down to a very rare farm right on the limits. It offers essential farm odours, the bizarre sight in these hills of cows and a single well-kept peacock which struts ambiguously on the roadside.

Here the limits get confusing in a knot of roads, unmarked military ones and settler roads with a profusion of signs in Hebrew and English. Roads which I discover later have very recently been opened to residents for the first time. I retreat, preferring to climb an accessible hill before me to the west. At the top I can see settler roads scarring the hill to the south and to the north the deep wadi that leads down to Ain Arik, a road I'm about to take myself. On the far side of this wadi is a grand hill, the westernmost peak of which carries a communication mast. I've climbed it before now, passing a manned security hut on top without notice and descended its very steep face to Ain Arik via a quarry full of roadblocks. Now I want to work my way down to the natural and profoundly unnatural form of limits at Bil'in.

The hill above Ain Arik first taught me how demanding these rough terraces can be but I make it down to the road to wait out the servees' rush hour race. One stops quite soon, opens onto cheery faces which encourage me to squeeze up front beside a beaming man from Kafr Nima. H is very keen to talk, marvels at my presence here, tries a flamboyant invitation to his home and is stunned when I accept. At Kafr Nima we get out and walk off to the far side of the village and his half-finished house where he lavishes me with as much attention as he can; apples, cucumbers, melon, water, finally coffee, which I accept before realising that he has only made it for me.

Meanwhile, I study the view that he details. Lowlands open out and roll down to Bil'in at the new 'border' or Occupation limits but it's far enough for haze to make for complication. So the place that H points to repeatedly, looks much larger and more built-up than I understood Bil'in could be. H is emphatic about it, in-between being emphatic about everything else; comically, sweetly so. He's even emphatic about accompanying me back to the main road, where he flags down a servee and plants four vigourous kisses on my cheeks.

At Bil'in the hills fade away and I find myself in a greatly spread out village that I cannot read and with no clear destination. I can't bring myself to ask for The Wall until befriending some boys who know exactly how to get there using short cuts through neighbouring properties and I'm on my way. As I leave the village behind I can see where the wall forms a point recognisable as Palestine's furthest extent now and one of confrontation. It's Monday, late afternoon, I am the only person here and can look harder and closer than if I'd come on a weekly Friday protest. It is quite a long walk to the olive groves ahead on a rising hillside topped by the Occupation wall and I'm feeling apprehensive. I want to go as far as I can, just don't know what it means as ever.

I keep on along a track through olives groves and low terracing, the ground blackened with scars of protest dispersal. I can see a security fence on the north and south, a gate or barrier up ahead more or less in front of me. Eery calm accompanies me to the barrier, which opens on to a classic patrol road; layers of fencing, electrified on the inside, clean lines. Up on the far hillside are some of the military's concrete shelters. It's from there that they emerge to start shooting at protesters on Fridays, especially since it's become an off-limits military zone here. There is no-one about today and I'm slightly stunned to be here, alone, able to nose around, unsure what to do!

I walk inside the layered limits and start to photograph it in case this moment is all I have. Down on my haunches to avoid the long shadow my body is making in lowering light, I can hear the scratchy interventions of a military radio. It is such a familiar sound somehow that I don't think much of it and stay focused on the layer of rubber grenades all over the ground at the barrier. Mixed in with them are canisters whose metal and size have caused severe, even fatal, injuries to people when shot directly at them here.

Crackling erupts behind me again. I turn and still see nothing, so turn back to absorb as much as possible. Crackles and vocal exchanges continue from the movie over the hill as I stand and trace the bizarre course that a patrol road and fencing takes across Palestinian farmland. It's numbingly familiar, this abusive non-sense. Up far ahead in the slowly rising hills is H's partly complete home with its sheltered entrance and weather worn walls and floors inside and out. I can't make it out but can see where it is on the ridge that extends from Kafr Nima. Now a loud crackling erupts and suddenly I realise what it is and that I don't know what happens if I am caught inside the limits.

I stand and decide to leave; do not want to condescend to these soldiers with explanations or politeness, so walk sharply away along the track. Within a hundred metres the accelerating tones of a military jeep approach around the hill towards where I've just been. I skip up on to the terrace into the sheltering olive trees and watch as the jeep draws up to where I was squatting, voices and crackling radio still audible, before it takes off on a patrol through the wall limits. This buys me some time so I explore the groves to see if I can reach the far fence and see beyond it.

As I step across the blackened ground—between a harvest of grenades, alone and gathered in small heaps with the brassy coloured canisters of fierce tear gas and repulsive smelling ones designed to linger on skin and clothes indeterminately—I wonder what the soldiers would expect me to do. What kind of damage might I do to their stupid fence system, whether that's what people do, whether it is what I'll do when I reach it this time. I feel a great desire to be predictable, but rolls of razor wire prevent me getting close enough to inflict token damage. I can see there is no view on offer; the point of Occupation here is to control space and deny sight.

Only when I've made my way back up into the hills am I able to reinterpret the view from H's roof. Now it is very clear what the Occupation wants to hide. The neat cluster of what looked more like a town than a village is not Bil'in, of course, but one part of a massive settlement built on recently stolen land beyond the barrier on the little hill of grenades I was standing on. It squats heavily over the ridge, just one part of Modi'in Illit which boasts of becoming the fourth largest city on the plains. The vulgarity of this Occupation that knows no limits is stunning to witness again.

The only possible response to it is raw outrage and clear-eyed appeals to justice. Crimes of this kind and scale ought not exist. When they do, they must be undone. When humanity errs to this extent over such sustained periods of time the response must be a corresponding justice on this earth, in our time. These are crimes against our humanity; against every one of us and everything that makes us civil beings. It falls to each of us to act by every means possible.

In Ramallah, running to the last, I reach my physical limits.

Running concentrates a sharp pain in my left calf muscle, strained in a distant wadi two days ago. Blissed-out, I'd looked up from the terrace to breath in the contoured rhythms and tripped on a loose rock. I winced and walked on for miles with only a badly grazed boot. Running is something else but I confront growing pain with even strides and calm constancy. What did the novelist say about pain and suffering? It's a hard run along al Tireh but I keep going to the end—and there it is!

Running in Ramallah has bound me to the place and set me against notions of space. Place is worn, freighted, complex. Space is seductive, abstract, dust-free. I'm running in an actual place, which is how I knew that George Habash Square exists. Many believe the sign has been removed, disallowed, banned but here it is: no-one surrendered. It's not marked on any map I own, except where I've written it myself. I half ran out here and there it was standing up against the settlements in the Palestinian hills. Square George Habash it reads and since there's no G as such in Arabic its got two J sounds. It's me that is running.

In Ramallah, I'm limping past a street sign. "Dalal Mughrabi (1958–1978) 'Born as a refugee in Lebanon in a family that was made a refugee from Yaffa in

1948. She joined FATAH and participated in a guerilla operation (Martyr Kamal Odwan Operation) with 12 others in occupied Palestine where she was killed.'" Hoping to ignite an uprising, she invested heavily. I only know enough about her to understand why she breached the limits, wonder what other ambitious 20 year old refugees think of her now.

In Ramallah, running doesn't dissolve the pain but heightens and hardens it. I struggle to limp most of the way back, past the guards and Lorca Street but at least I get to pay witness. At the end of the ridge this morning it was clear enough to see Yaffa beyond Bil'in and the vast white cities below. It's almost as distinct as the view from Deir Ghassanah in the north, on the hill where their shahids are honoured. Words matter, everywhere.

Walking in Nablus, I admired the spontaneous memorials which have turned into a bureaucratic process in Ramallah. That is; a rehearsal for nationhood. Funny how a sign at George Habash Square is meaningless until it no longer exists. Funny again, altogether, in the coming Palestine. It's me that was running, no more.

In Ramallah 2010.

Within Limits, None.

I'm returning again to the hill with no reliable name, which harbours the remains of the nation's poet and will soon give form to his memorial building. The hill which holds so much of Ramallah's municipal waste that it forms a plateau of its own on the south-east side and will soon give form to another new suburb. The hill which stretches southwards above land snatched by Occupation; walled, fenced, sliced up, armed, imprisoned, in abrogation of International law and basic humanity and will soon, someday, eventually give form to a new Palestine.

Returning to a hill which possesses an unlikely clustering of conifers, rings of more or less abandoned terraces and two or three Bedouin families' improvised dwellings, but will soon make rich non-resident Palestinian investors richer. The hill that I visited on my Day of Memorials and borrowed the poet's epitaph from his gravestone. Walking with varying versions of those words for two days before settling on their original form: "in/on this earth there is something to live for". Words or a phrase that lingered in a way that had me bearing witness to the witness bearer.

Returning with something very different in mind this morning; to find caves in the hill that rebels of other ages and resistance fighters of the most recent intifada used as a refuge from various Occupiers. Returning some potency to this particular place. These caves are difficult to find, I'm told, but "if you keep looking you'll find them".

I turn up to the terrace below the trees off the road to Rafat, up and along. I have sandals and shorts on but am welcomed graciously by the entire family of thistles. So I step carefully, lightly, deliberately, unadventurously around the hillside on this enchanted early morning. A Bedouin woman watches me from below, puzzling and silent. I take each step seriously, like a rebel laying down words. Like a poet loading their gun. Like a hill offering refuge.

This hill has been so many things to me already, from beginning to end. Yet I've seen so many hills here that I've wanted to befriend and defend with my words. How potent can one hill be? It contains the body of the poet, the poet of the nation, the soul of Palestine, and portals to the future, the coming liberation. The return of a radically new place in space of Occupation. A return to the old place within a radically new one. Poetic, physical and political ellipses come together in a three dimensional manifestation of what the philosopher conjures with his island of Impotential.

I tread precisely around, up and down, checking and picking up on a Bedouin pathway to verify that blue tarpaulins suspended over rocky terraces do not disguise cave entrances. Passing animal enclosures and a big bank of beehives, where that dreadful collective burring speeds me on. Out, up, down and around to familiar sights before the Jerusalem Hills; Rafat's charms, military prison and shooting range, sewage and a still silent dump. My footsteps stitch up a dramatic story of wounds over the rear of Ramallah.

Z told me first of resistance caves up in a wide valley to the north beyond Jibiya where I walked and before a major clustering of settlements. Used over the ages against varying invaders and during the recent long-sustained defence of Nablus. These are tranquil wadis and perfect hideouts, near the most maltreated parts of the Palestinian Hills. Then I hear of these ones and others very close to Ramallah, places

I know too. As potent and heartening as all of them are to me, as much as they redefine these over-defined limits once more, this is the hill I most want to find rebel caves in.

I divert to every rock of any scale or notable formation, wonder if the caves are now buried below the dump? Whether the developers I met wandering over the plot they're interested in buying here knew of them? My legs are wearing fresh blood again and yet I won't mind if I don't find any caves. Even if I do, I realise that I cannot and anyway will not reveal their location. I won't even confirm their existence. To do so would remove their greatest value, which is to introduce doubt into the minds of the victorious, as the poet wrote.

The Bookman described caves in the northerly limits, near to where his family have farmed for generations, where he went as a boy for the season; grapes, figs, olives—months at a time. Where he remembers early settlers coming and shooting at them during harvest. One is not far from George Habash Square, others are invested in wadis below. These wadis, layering north, always stir-up words and images of the poet's produced after he was able to return. "I am a child of mountains and stability", he lamented on seeing the effects of decades of Occupation. Then in a long poem he writes of how "instead of being shielded by them" now he has to "shield" or protect these same hills. The inversions are many and grotesque.

These caves in these hills are within limits, they are thresholds. They offer a new form of sanctuary, albeit potential, in the same old hills that cannot offer it naturally anymore. Nothing is quite so simple and yet there is potency in the thought. There is hope beyond the end of Raja'a Street. Now I understand more fully how life is possible in or on this particular earth and walk away mindfully; no longer running but still fired up. The thunking of earth movers has begun and trucks have arrived at the dump. Morning is unfolding and the potency of the hill remains intact.

I greet the guard at the poet's gravestone for a last time and we discuss the only thing we can between languages; the Mondial. We share our glee about seeing previous and usual winners being knocked out, hopes of a real shake-up. I'm allergic to football but have been rooting with new friends for this different future, seeing it getting very close under the stars at Beit Aneeseh. I tell him that I want Slovenia, Algeria or Ghana to win and we laugh excitedly and in unison.

Within limits, there are also none.

Accompanying artworks by Paul Noble.
Family is Infinity (or Hard Labour), 2011, p. 39
Cathedral, 2011, p. 55.
This is The Way, 2011, p. 79.
Courtesy the artist and Gagosian Gallery.

1 Of course, numbers do have peculiar and dreadful stories and significance in Palestine; '37, '48, '67, '71, '87, '93, 2000, 2008....

In Ramallah, on the Border
Adania Shibli

In Ramallah, on the Borders

Adania Shibli

After I finished hanging the last curtain in the house, I lay on the bed and began to howl, then the neighbour's dog on the opposite hill began to howl too. It was after midnight when I realised how much I hate this city, Ramallah.

Before realising this, I had cleaned the house well. I had dusted the furniture, mopped the floor, re-laundered the sheets and towels, and re-washed most of the dishes, despite that the house had already been cleaned. The landlord told me they brought someone especially to clean, still there's no harm in making sure it is. And I had rented this house a few days ago, immediately after moving here to start my new job. The job is good and the house is good. However, all this would probably not prevent my gradual loss of self-confidence and the sense of isolation in this vile city.

Regardless, as I woke the next morning I was struck by a feeling of satisfaction, the sole source of which was the cleanliness of the house, and perhaps the new curtains hung on its windows. I had also placed my glass table next to the biggest window, where I would sit every morning before going to work. I would drink my coffee there as well, while the neighbours' three children would pass by and say hello, which would prompt the feeling of a peaceful life overlooking a backyard that can be seen by no one. For generally in Ramallah there are clear borders between things, and observing them so that everything remains within its limits, leads to two things. On the one hand, it leads to a great respect that feeds one's feeling of self satisfaction upon which one could build one's whole life, and, on the other hand, to a complete emptiness. The result is an empty life that enjoys everyone's respect. Yet, few are those who have succeeded in perfecting moving within these borders without overstepping them, and I am not one of them. As soon as I see a border, either I run quickly over it, or I stealthily cross it by one step. But I do not think that such behaviour is totally conscious or that there is an existential impulse behind it; it is, rather, the result of clumsiness. It is a kind of handicap. Thus, and in order to avoid the fear, pain, and suffering that might result from my transgression of borders, I decided that while in Ramallah I would try as much as possible to stay within the borders of my house. However, as the house has many windows, including a big one through which my neighbours and their three children could see me and thus see me crossing borders even while in my own house, I had hung curtains. Sometimes, though, I would forget to close them, but since I am usually alone when I am in the house, I would just sit at my glass table and stare at the horizon. So this is all that the neighbours' kids would see of me, to the degree that when I would one day travel and disappear for a few days, the middle one would tell me after my return that he had missed seeing me every morning sitting at my table.

I know it might seem to some that I am exaggerating in my description of things, but this is precisely the problem that I just described; I often lose the ability to distinguish the borders between things, and thus misjudge them more than people normally do. For instance, when a military patrol stops us and the soldier opens the door and I see the barrel of his rifle, I go crazy, from fear I think. So I ask him to move it aside while talking to me or asking to see my ID Then the people around me start to grumble about my exaggerated reaction, for according to them there is no need to create such tension; the soldier will not shoot me, and even if he did, my reaction would not change anything. Yes, I might understand that, but not in the moment; only hours, or days, or even years later. That is just an example, but the principle itself could apply to everything, from taking off some clothes while being searched at a checkpoint, to asking about the price of a filthy and rotten head of wilted lettuce from an amateur greengrocer at the Ramallah vegetable market. And I stress the word amateur, because he is sitting in the middle of the closed market on a

Friday asking three times the price of a normal head of lettuce. The problem again, as I have said, is that I lack the ability to judge things rationally, so often such events really affect me. They shake me to my core, to the point that I no longer recognise what is permitted and what is not, which then pushes me to transgress borders even more so than before.

Yet once again, all of this fear, pain, and suffering resulting from my inability to recognise and respect the logical borders between things subsides in solitude. So better to stay alone within the borders of my house, where I sit at my table every day and watch what appears of this empty city through my big window, that is those pine trees on the opposite hill playing tirelessly with the horizon. I sit there daily before I go to my new job, which will remain new for me until the end of my contract, for I do not know at which moment it is supposed to turn from being my new job, into just being my job. And I often stay there until late at night, later even than the night guard's ability to stay awake, therefore I have been given my own key and was taught the alarm code, which is easy to remember: 5391. And I stay at work late because I often arrive at the office late. This is because the neighbours' stupid and annoying dog usually wakes me at night, after which I cannot get back to sleep until the start of the dawn prayer call. So I wake up late and arrive to work late, where I stay late before going back home and sleep immediately, until the neighbours' dog wakes me again.

By the way, I hope I did not disclose an uncomfortable secret when I mentioned the soldier or the checkpoint, or when I announce, for example, that normal life here is under Occupation. The sound of bullets, the military patrols' sirens, sometimes the fighter planes, helicopters, and bombardments, followed by the sirens of ambulances, not only rival the howling of the dog, but also always come just minutes before the breaking news banner on the TV screen. Things have been like this for so long that many of those still alive cannot remember the minor details of life before then, such as a rotten head of lettuce being offered for sale in the vegetable market on the day it is closed. Instead, things such as killing are the daily matters, or, let us say, happen in this context, so often, in fact, that I'm usually indifferent to them. Seriously. For example, one rainy morning I woke up really late and went straight to work. When I got out of the shared taxi, I noticed that the street was empty, and that there was a military patrol stationed near al-Bandi's despicable grocery store. But this was nothing out of the ordinary, so I continued in the opposite direction towards my work. When I got to the top of the street that leads to my office, a pedestrian pointed out to me that the area was under curfew and that the army had surrounded one of the nearby buildings. In this also I found nothing out of the ordinary, and I continued on my way to work. There in the middle of the street, in front of the main gate of the building where my office is, I saw two soldiers standing. Having finally learned to keep calm and maintain high spirits on such occasions, I waved to them while smiling, and shouted that I work in the building they were standing in front of. At that moment one of them got down on the ground and placed his hand on his left knee, pointing the barrel of his rifle at me, and I jumped to the nearby fig tree to shield myself with its branches from shots that never came.

While it may have been inappropriate or unkind of the soldier to point his rifle at me, I understood what he meant. I needed to find a different way to get to work, since until now there was nothing so unusual as to force me to go home. Indeed, I easily jumped over the walls and borders between the houses, and I think breaching borders in this case was completely justified, no? And finally, I arrived at work.

Since only three of my colleagues had made it to the office that day, I worked well and efficiently without being disturbed by anyone until, that is, one of those colleagues came and opened my office window without my permission. When I protested, he said that the glass would shatter if he did not open it. The army had warned the residents of the neighbourhood that they were going to blow up the neighbouring building that they had surrounded with the three young men in it who had refused to surrender. And that is precisely what happened a few minutes later. That colleague had forgotten to open one of the windows, the glass of which shattered. Still, the result of his opening my office window was unbearable. Moments after the explosion, which literally shook the entire building, there erupted a thick cloud of dust, some of which landed on my papers and even on my hand that was holding the pen. I had to stop working. I cannot stand dust at all, especially this coarse dust that generates a creeping sound when papers covered in it touch, or when my pen comes into contact with them. It was only after I cleaned the office of it thoroughly that I was able to get back to my work.

Actually, it may occur to some that my behaviour is a response to the call to confront the culture of power with the power of culture, i.e. that it reflects a desire to hold on to life despite the attempts of the Occupation to destroy it, or the insistence that there is that which deserves life on this earth, at least in Ramallah. Nonsense. There is no relationship at all between my behaviour and such a belief, for my attachment to my job is not only related to disasters produced by the occupier, but also to those produced by nature. One day there was a heavy snowfall that forced the majority of my colleagues to leave the office quickly, before the snow started accumulating on the roads stopping traffic. I, however, stayed at work, but not because I love my job.

All there is to it all is that I'm unable to determine the borders between things, and therefore not being able to evaluate things logically, so I usually see the fly's shit on the painting instead of the painting itself. For all that a person like me notices or remembers of a city as old and storied as Ramallah, with its municipal council more than one hundred years old, is that disgusting head of wilted lettuce for sale in the Ramallah vegetable market on the one day of the week that the market is closed, or of the bombing of a building next door, with three young men inside it, only the dust that follows.

Some, though, might say that this way of looking at things, which involves focusing on the most trivial and minor details—be it the shit of the fly on the painting, the rotten head of lettuce in Ramallah's vegetable market, or the dust on the table after the building's bombing—is not only the absolute proof of the truth but also the only way of arriving at it. In an old story that historian Carlo Ginzburg retells, three brothers meet a man who has lost his camel. Immediately, the three brothers describe the missing camel to the man: it was white and one-eyed, had two bags on its saddle, one full of oil and the other wine. The man shouts that they must have seen it. No, they answer, they have not. But the man does not believe them and accuses them of having stolen his camel. The four are brought before the court, where the three brothers prove their innocence after revealing to the judge how from the smallest traces and simplest details they were able to accurately describe an animal they had never actually seen.

The truth here, without the need for long and careful observation nor an intense life experience in Ramallah to arrive at it, is that in a city that sells rotten lettuce for a king's ransom, a city that is covered by the dust of destruction, and a city that claims that there is that which deserves life inside it, yet is obsessed with respecting borders, there is no need to see anything or do anything other than to hide in an office behind one's desk, or in one's house behind the curtains hung in front of the large window. For how tolerant of the transgression of borders is solitude in Ramallah. In fact, it makes living in this city alright.

An excerpt from a novel in progress. Translated by Christopher Stone.

Ramallah Versus Ramallah

Najwan Darwish

> How did I not notice them building the walls? But I didn't hear the din of the workers, not a single sound. Constantine Cavafy

In a poem by Cavafy called "Walls", he describes a person who finds himself surrounded by walls. He doesn't know how they could have been built without his noticing them. As for me, I know how these walls were built around our lives.

I am now sitting in the dark to look at Ramallah, a city I've long been angry with because of its status as a symbol of an odious political period: the Oslo period.

In the second half of the 1990s Ramallah became the capital of Palestinian self-rule. Quickly, ministries were improvised, along with six security services, Arafat's compound (where he would die of poisoning, a Shakespearean ending after ten years), the Governate of Ramallah, the villas occupied by new officials with security stations in front, and the poor soldiers on the sides of the road. The word "returnee"—different from the idea of return so deeply ingrained in us—spread and eventually lost any meaning. Millions of refugees remained in their places of refuge. It was the leadership that had "returned", along with a few thousand soldiers and bureaucrats. New kinds of NGOs sprung up like mushrooms, a result of the deluge of foreign funding meant to support the current political process—"the peace process". It was a new phase, one with its own symbols and values that brutally eclipsed those of the 1987 Intifada, as well as all of its lessons, sacrifices and hopes. This new phase also had its own confused cultural and artistic scene: there was a great effort to flee to the future, to leap over the facts on the ground as well as what is owed to history. It was a kind of coma that the victim goes into, until he or she feels no more pain.

In that period in particular, i.e. the post-Oslo period, we came to know the "checkpoints", the "permits", the "Valley of Hell" road, and the carving up of land. The idea of separating us from our geography entered a new phase. Some generals sat around a table and decided that the Palestinian presence was a cancer that had to be removed. The first stage of treatment required besieging every "Palestinian population centre", at first so that the cancerous cells would not grow, but with the ultimate goal of the annihilation of Palestine as a society. Colonial urban planning undertook the mission. This is how the Occupation viewed its "partners in peace". It built by-pass roads exclusively for the settlers who would no longer have to go through Palestinian towns to get to their settlements, the building and expansion of which reached a fevered zenith under Sharon's segregation plan. The Zionist project was at the height of its rapaciousness in terms of the theft of land and the erasure of its people. It used the Palestinian "entity" to destroy the idea of Palestine and to legitimate the Occupation. "Palestine" came to mean everything but Palestine. It was in those years that Ramallah began to blossom as a 'city' in the same way that Amman has: the desecration of nature, the absence of urban planning and the predominance of slapdash building: buildings going up and up and projects in full swing, not to mention the population creep towards Ramallah from every corner of the 'West Bank' because of the job opportunities, the presence of the PA, and all of that "doner" money.

Writings from the first half of the twentieth century describe Ramallah as a village subordinate to Jerusalem. Khalil al-Sakakini (1878–1963) writes in one of his articles from the 1920s, for example: "in the morning we passed through the village of Ramallah". In the second half of the century, however, it expanded as a result of the fleeing to it of 1948 refugees, many of whom went not to the Am'ari, Jalazone, Kadourah, and Qalandia refugee camps, but rather settled in the village itself, which quickly became a town alongside its neighbour al-Bireh. The two together would become something of a centre. Ramallah had a reputation as a summer destination in the 1950s and 1960s when the 'West Bank' was under Jordanian authority, i.e. from the beginning of the 1950s to 1967. One remembers the black and white photos of King Hussein's visit to Ramallah, and Samira Tawfik's rustic song "Where? To Ramallah", that was popular back then.

"Qalandia" during "Jordan time" as we call it, was the name of a small airport. It was Jerusalem's airport from which one could travel to Cairo, Beirut, and Baghdad. In the "peace process" phase, in the area of the old airport, "Qalandia" became the name of the checkpoint that separates Ramallah from the rest of the world. I will forget much about the Occupation, but I'll never forget the long hours of waiting at the Qalandia checkpoint, the days in which those both leaving and entering Ramallah felt 'crucified' by the wait to get through. The sounds of car horns, the mayhem, and the hellish design of the checkpoint robs people of their humanity over time, as do the muddy puddles in the winter, the deadly summer afternoons, the growth of the checkpoint, the perfection of its techniques of suffering, and the stories of the tortuous wait of those trying to enter or leave Ramallah.

Ramallah has never been lucky. Its choice to be a "temporary capital" after Oslo is like a ten year old girl "choosing" to be a mother: it's a kind of rape, yet another act of colonial violence in a larger colonial project to re-engineer Palestinian identity and memory. It is an attempt to invent a new kind of Palestinian, a Palestinian without history and without memory, all for the benefit of the history and memory of the coloniser. The image of Ramallah was inflated—filled with air—to eclipse the Palestinian idea of it, to be a "new Palestine". It was meant not only to make us forget Jaffa, Haifa, Acre, the Galilee, and all of Palestine that was occupied in 1948, but also to overshadow the importance of Jerusalem. The new centrality of Ramallah has come as another blow to Jerusalem's critical position among Palestinians, along with the segregation regime with its physical manifestations such as wall, the checkpoints, and the occupiers' laws. A new Palestinian 'age' has dawned: "the age of Ramallah". We should have resisted the colonial designs on our identity and memory. I'm against Ramallah when the Occupation wants it be a "reservation for indigenous peoples". I'm against this cage woven by the wall. I'll love it again when this big lie is exposed. I have a feeling, akin to a vision, that I'll pass by

Qalandia one day and the checkpoint and the wall will have disappeared. It will have become an area of green, safe and relaxing public gardens. I'll see a woman pushing a stroller and children playing nearby, children from a generation that has not seen what we have seen. At that time I'll try to forget. Only then will I try.

Summer 2011. Translated by Christopher Stone.

Artists' Works

In Ramallah, Running
Francis Alÿs

Project of covering with gold leaf
the Eastern side of the West Bank wall

Francis Alÿs
Gold Leaf Project,
Palestine, 2005.
Courtesy the artist.

Francis Alÿs
Gold Leaf Project,
Palestine, 2005.
Courtesy the artist.

Project of covering with gold leaf
the western side of the West Bank wall

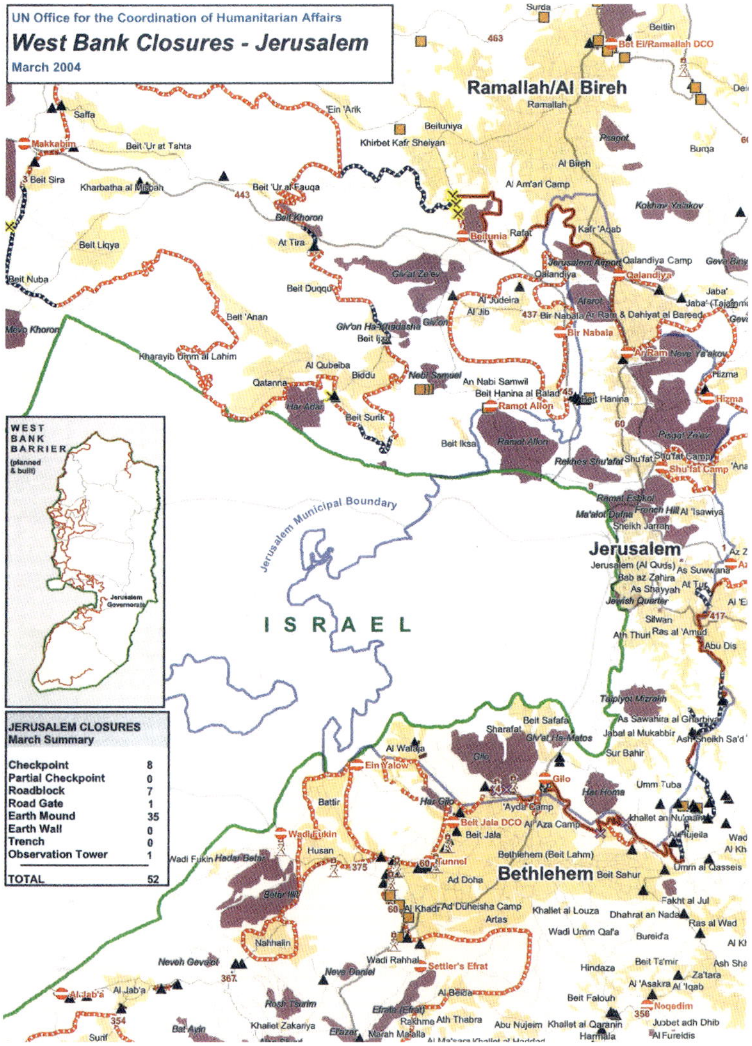

Francis Alÿs
Gold Leaf Project,
Palestine, 2005.
Courtesy the artist.

Francis Alÿs
Gold Leaf Project,
Palestine, 2005.
Courtesy the artist.

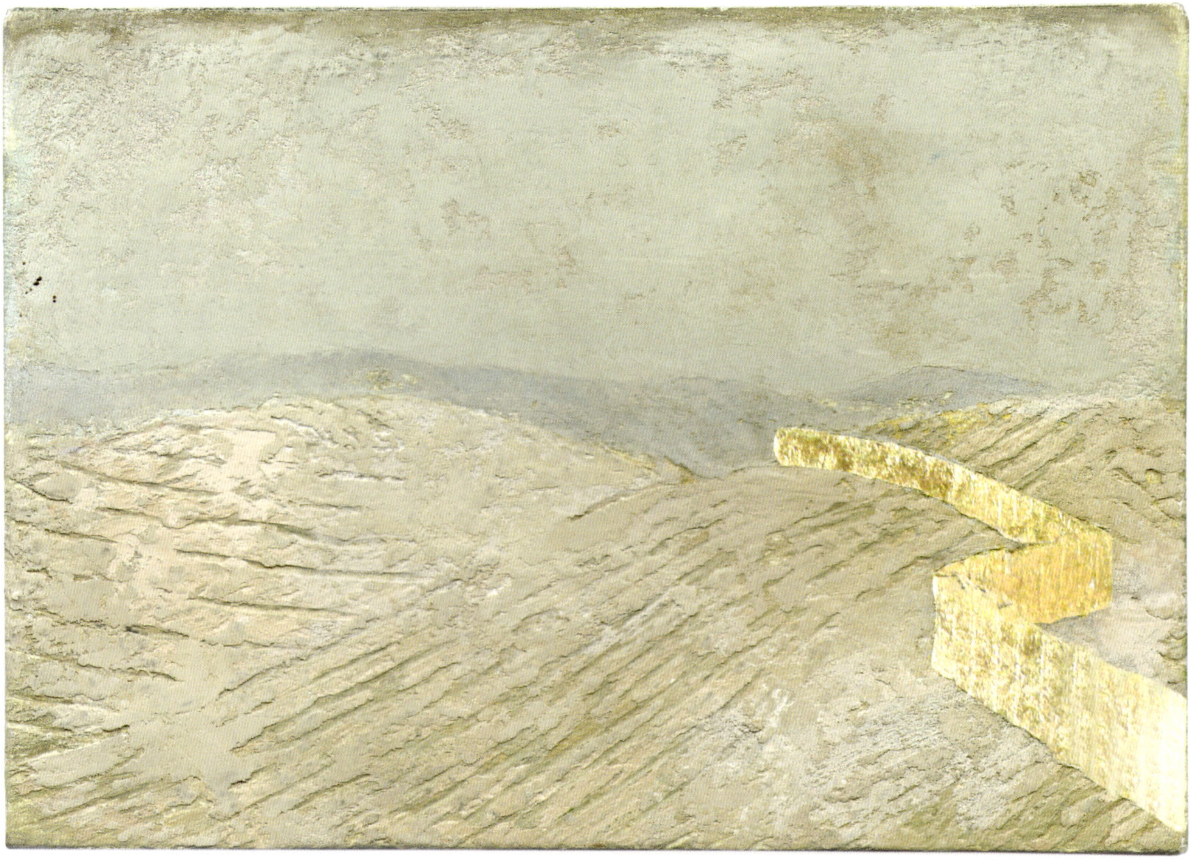

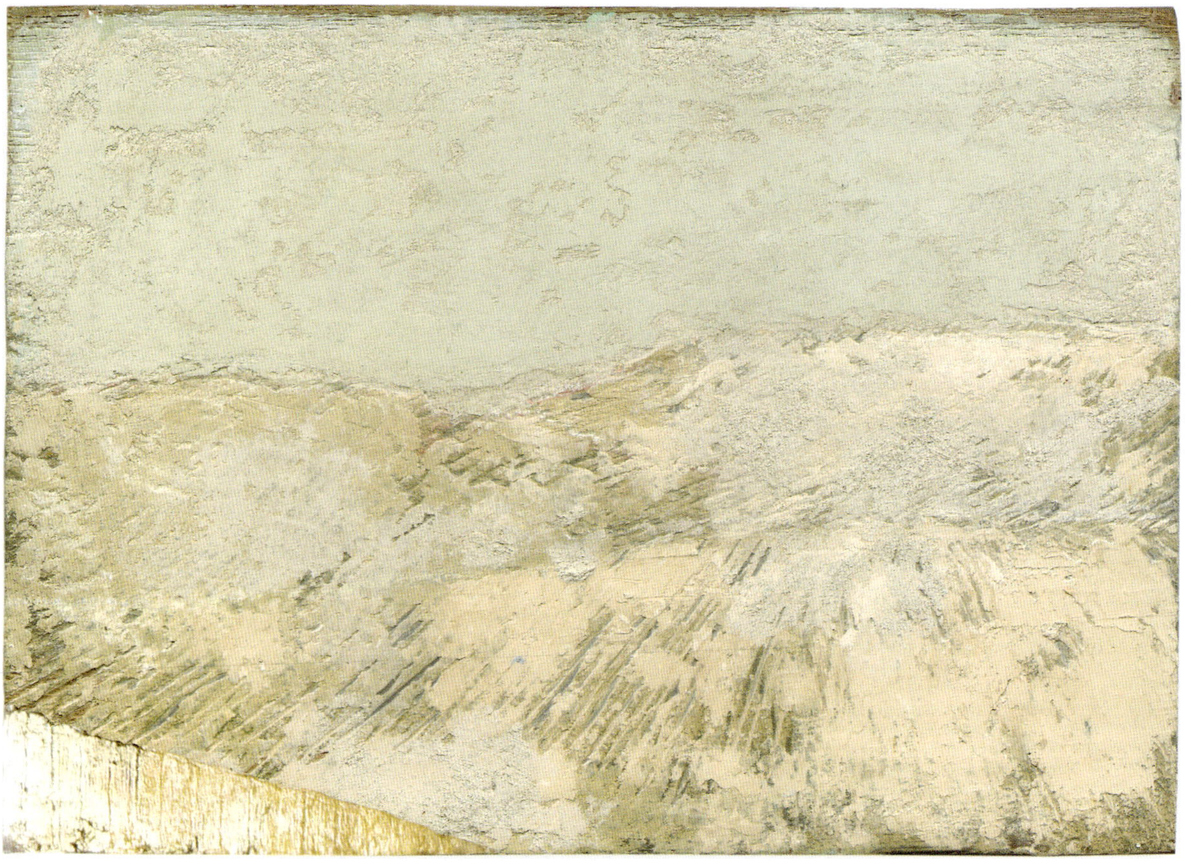

Jananne al-Ani
City, 2011.
Courtesy the artist.

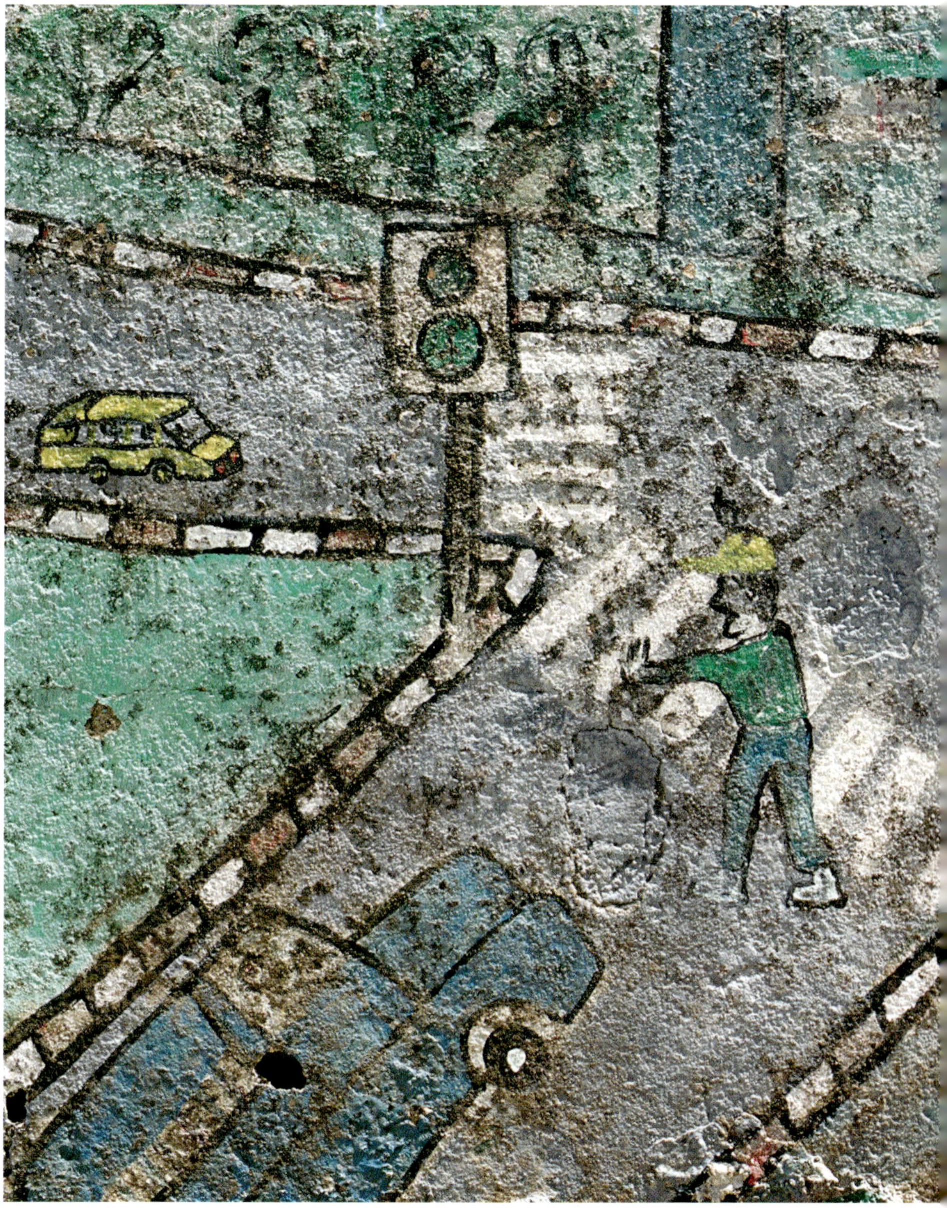

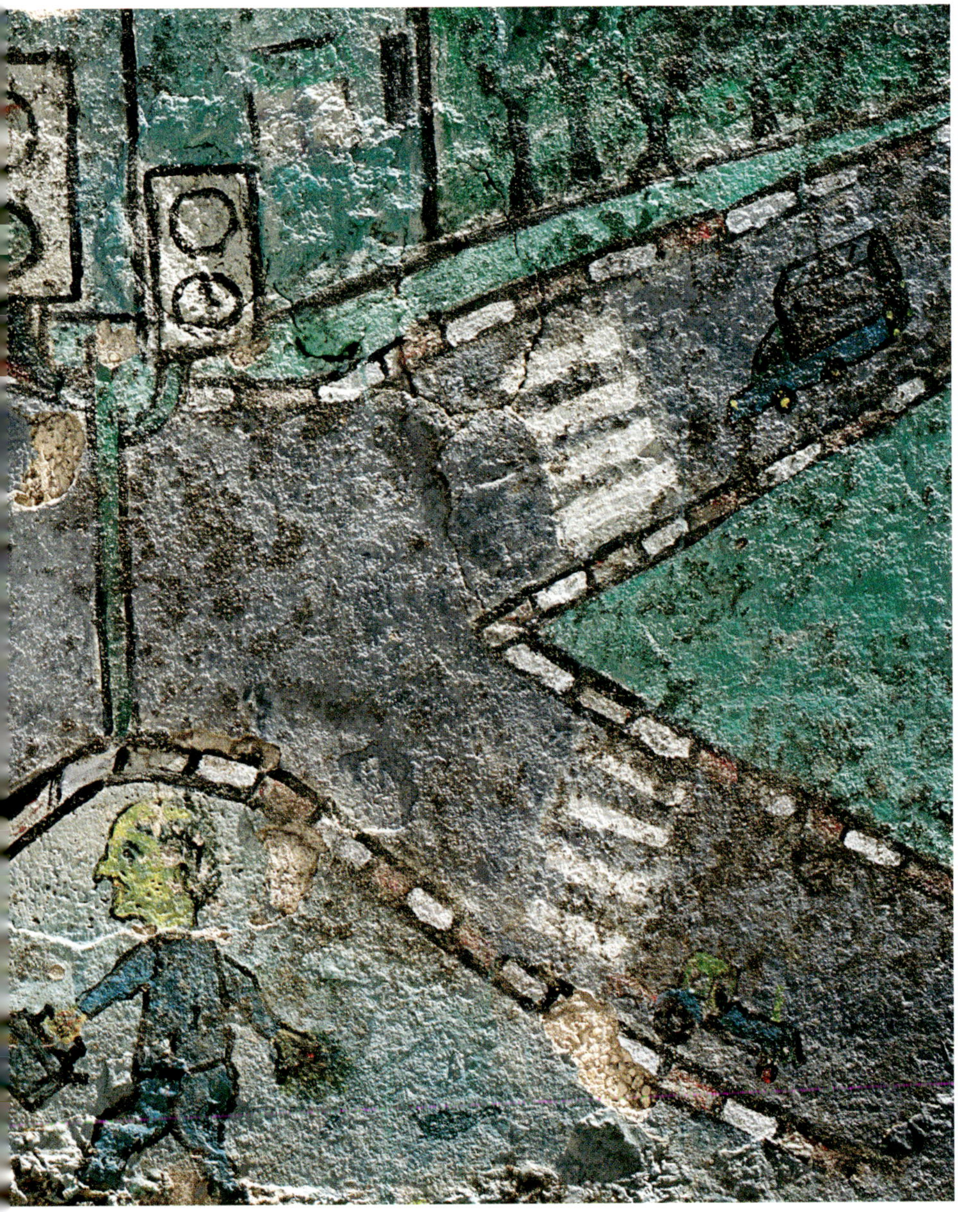

Jananne al-Ani
Country I, 2011.
Courtesy the artist.

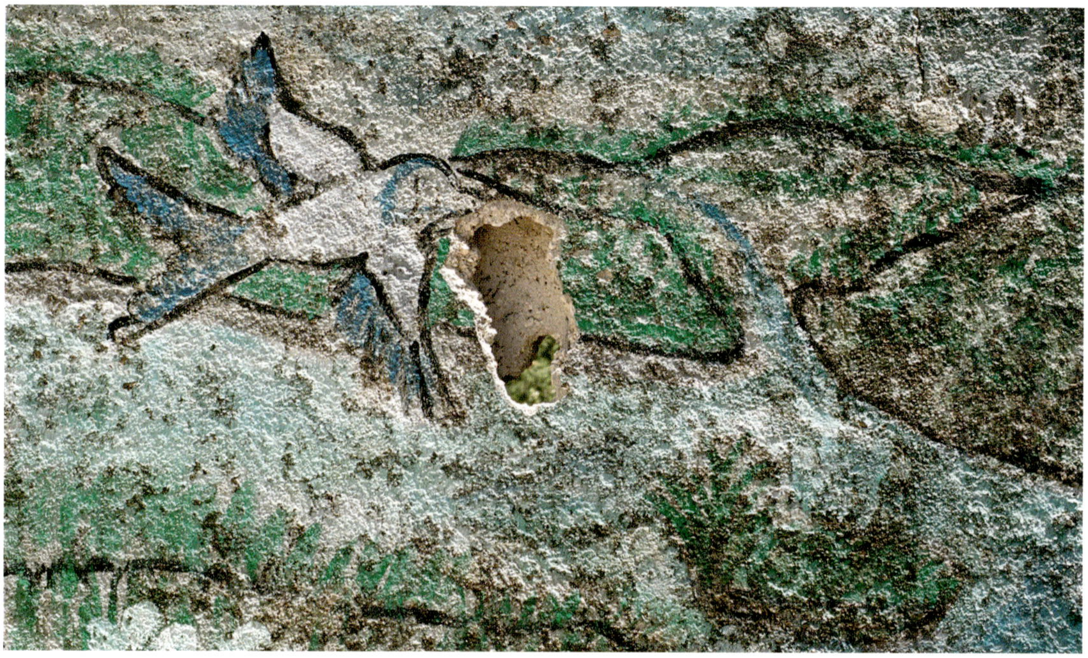

Jananne al-Ani
Country II, 2011.
Courtesy the artist.

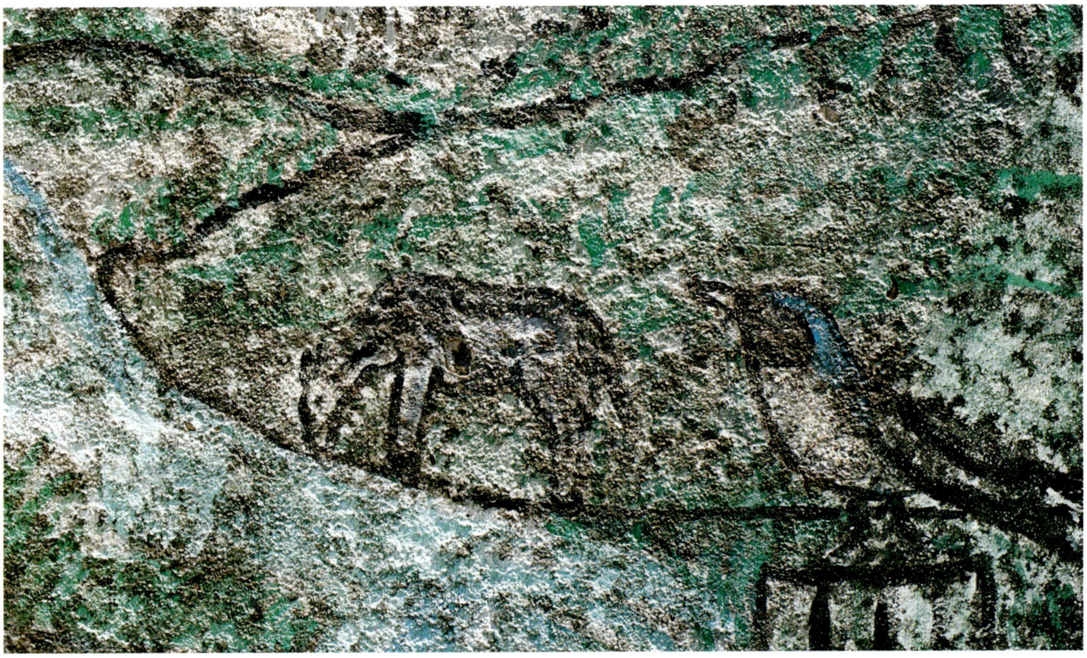

& Right

Right &

Khalil Rabah
Right and Right, 2000.
Courtesy the artist.

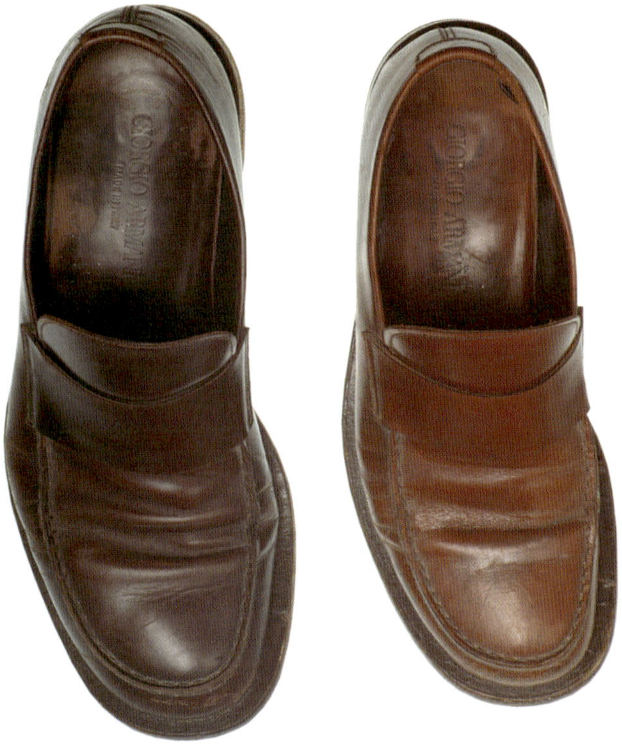

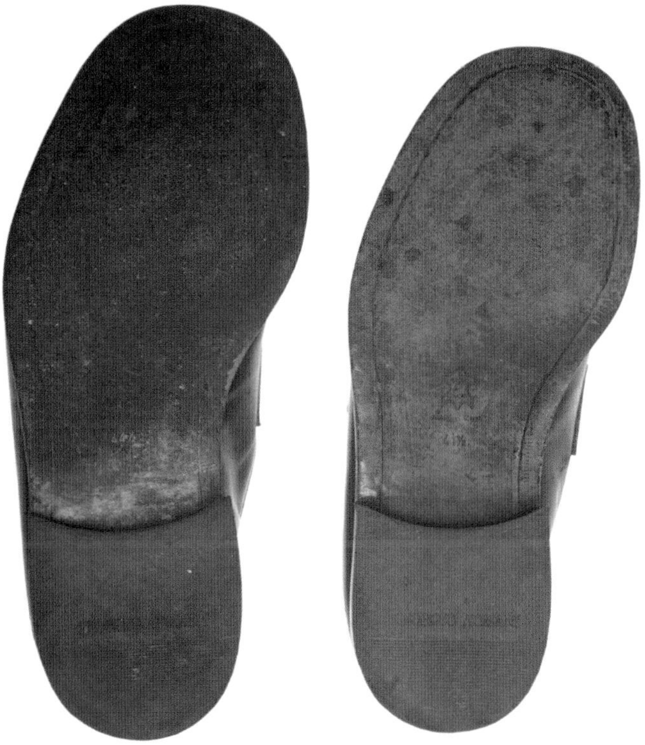

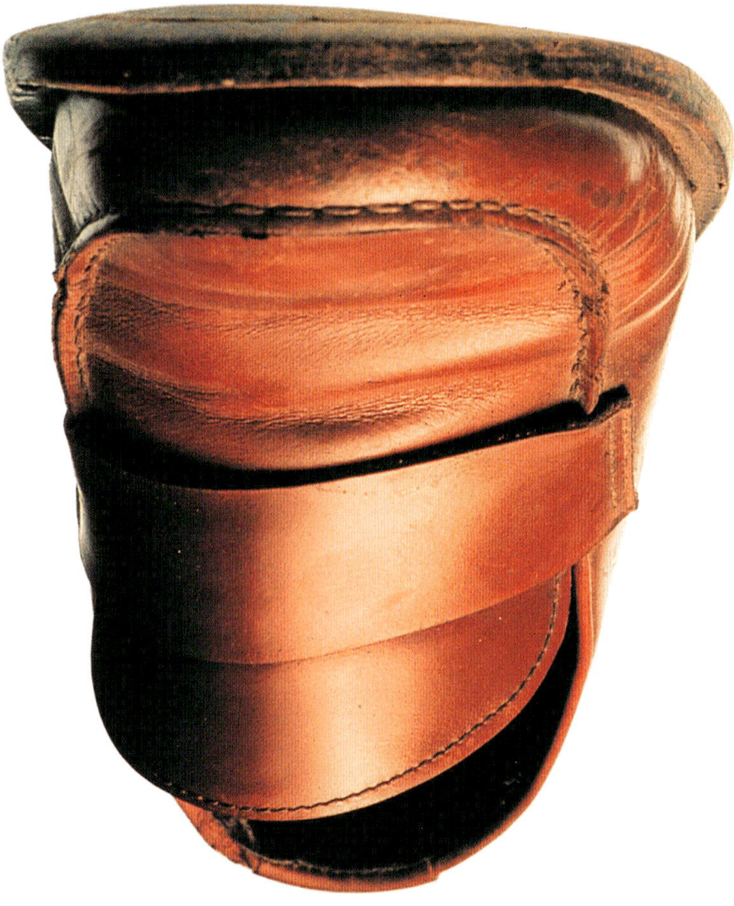

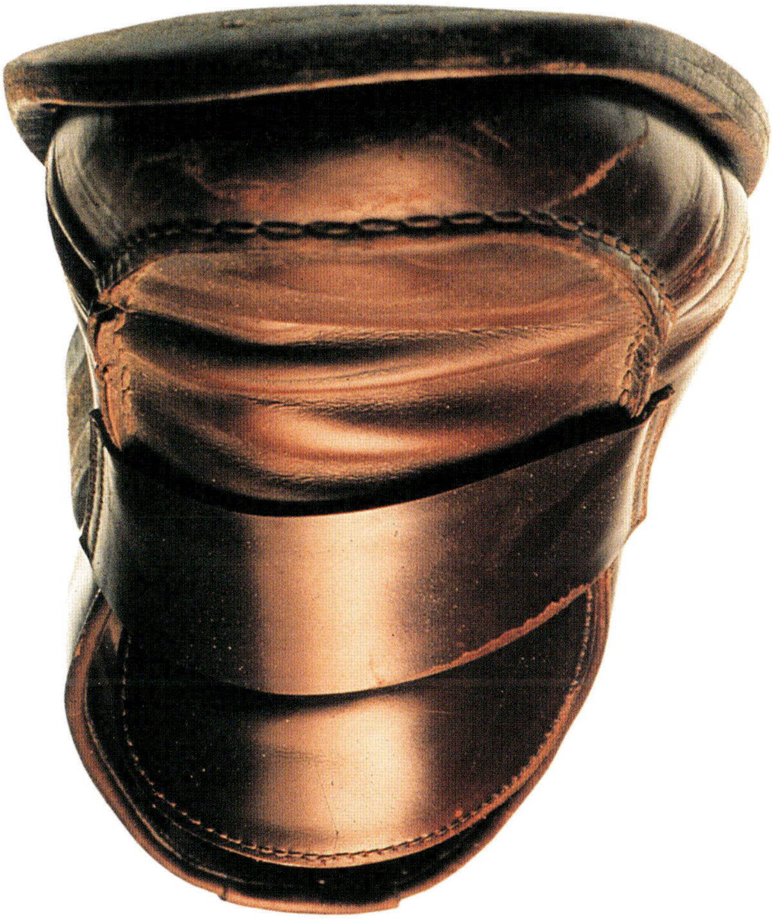

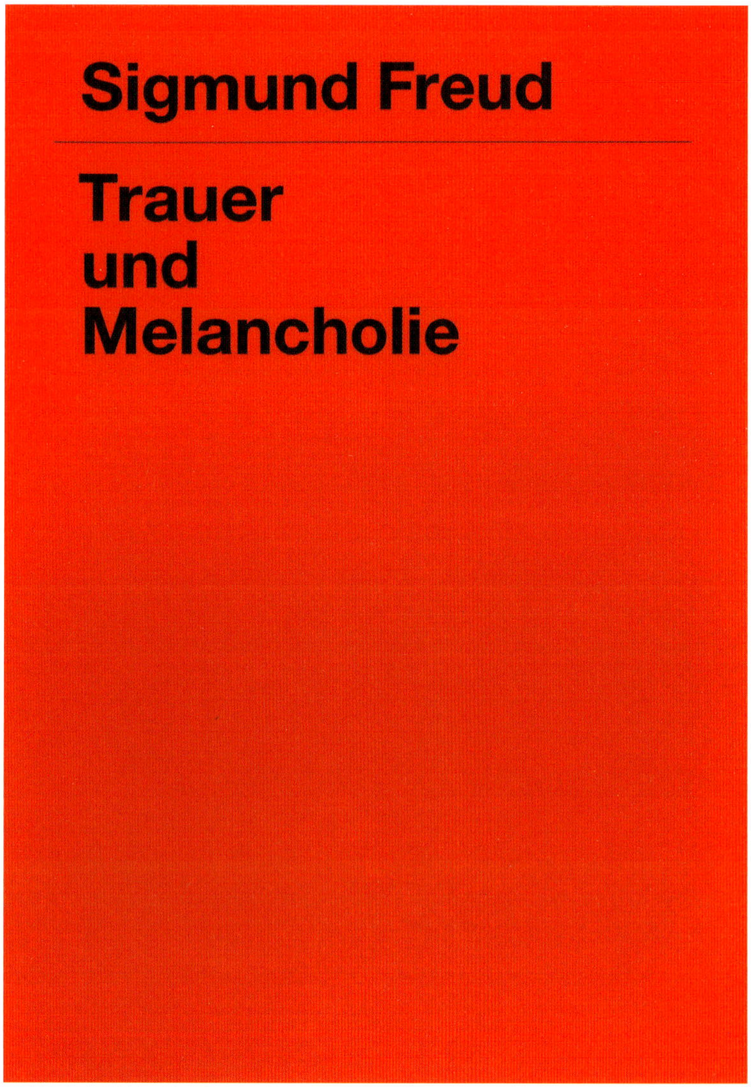

Olaf Nicolai
Sigmund Freud, Mourning and Melancholia (German), 2011.
Courtesy the artist.

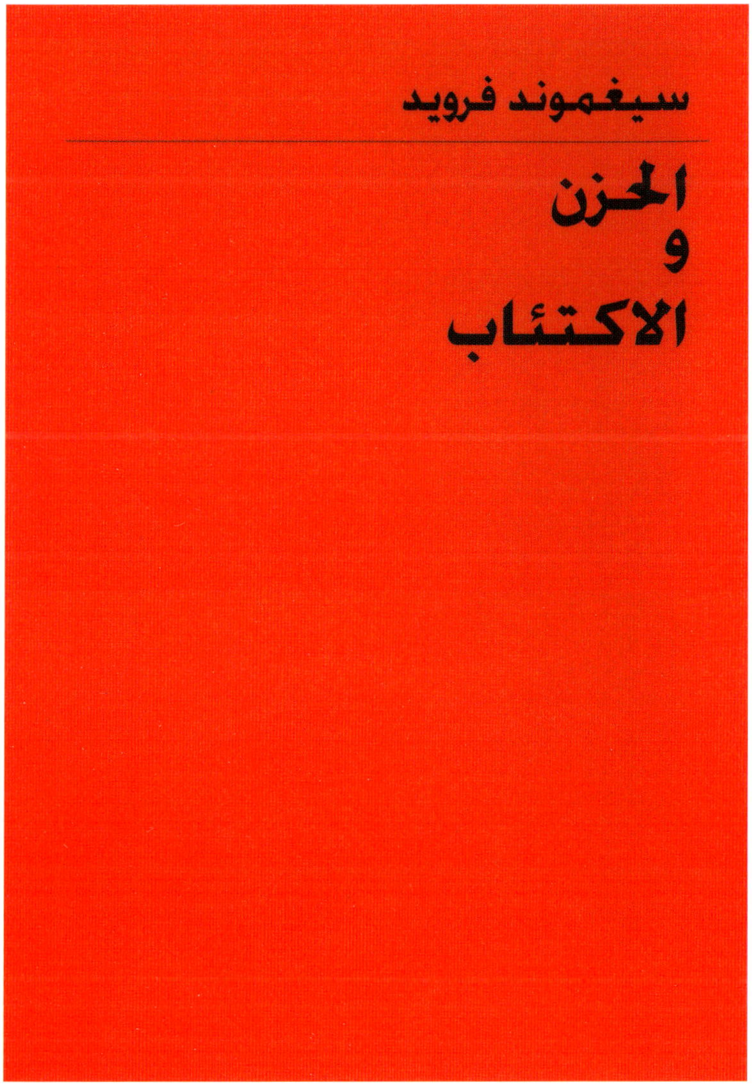

Olaf Nicolai
Sigmund Freud, Mourning and Melancholia (Arabic), 2011.
Courtesy the artist.

Olaf Nicolai
Publicity material for the broadcast of *Mourning and Melancholia*, 2009.
Courtesy the artist.

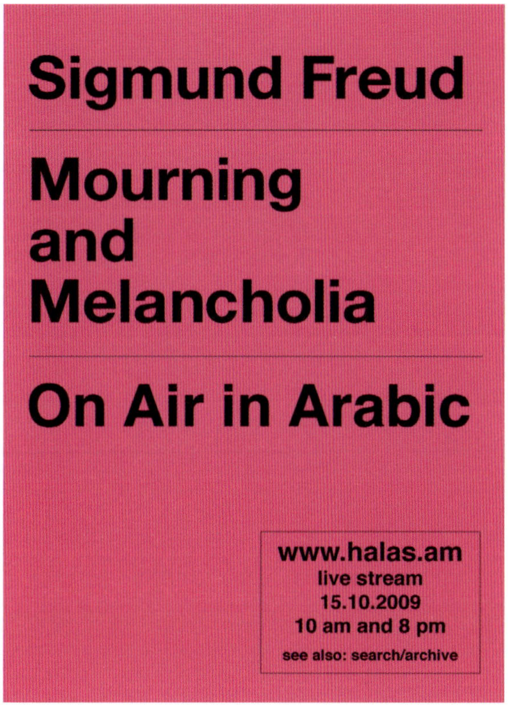

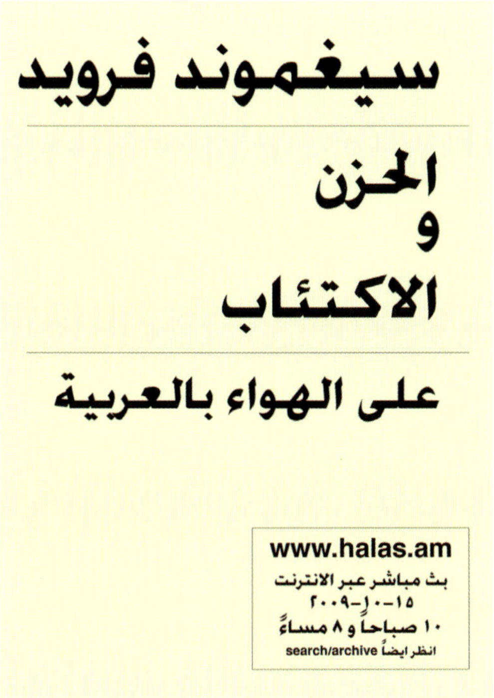

Olaf Nicolai
Statement, 2011.
Courtesy the artist.

MOURNING AND MELANCHOLIA

I visited the West Bank and Ramallah for the first time in 2007, following an invitation by Charles Esche, Director of the Van Abbe Museum in Eindhoven. A Biennial for contemporary art was planned and visiting artists were asked to propose works for this exhibition. My proposal was to translate and publish a text by Sigmund Freud that didn't yet exist in Arabic: *Mourning and Melancholia*.

Freud began work on this text—which deals with the two basic psychological mechanisms to handle the loss of objects—six months after the start of the First World War and finished it in May 1915.

Several reasons led to the choice of this particular text. Palestinian psychoanalyst Gehad Marzaweh mentioned in a conversation during my researches that it is important for him in relation to the current situation in the Middle East. Marzaweh grew up Palestinian in Israel until the age of 20. For 33 years he has been practicing in his ownmedical office, currently situated in Freiburg/Breisgau. His psychoanalytic practice focuses on work with trauma patients and traumatised victims of torture.

Another reason to choose this text lies in my own biography. I grew up in the GDR, where it was forbidden to publish writings by Sigmund Freud until the 1980s. *Mourning and Melancholia* was the title of the first selection of Freud's essays to appear in 1982.

An Arabic translation of this text was made available as a self-made booklet and given away free at different places in Ramallah and Birzeit University. In addition, an audio version in the local dialect was produced and broadcasted through the local radio station AMWAJ Radio. 91.5 FM. The project was realised with support by the Goethe-Institute in Ramallah and in cooperation with Thyssen-Bornemisza Art Contemporary on the occasion of the third Riwaq Biennial in Autumn 2010.

The work was conceived against the background of the very marginal circulation of Freud's writings in Arabic and the ongoing discussion about the relevance of psychoanalysis in the Arabic world, but equally implies questions regarding the function of translation in the context of apolitics of language where the distinction between Literary Arabic and the local vernacular is virulent.

Above all, the work aims at establishing mutual points of reference and rehearsing a space beyond antagonistic positions.

Olaf Nicolai

Mark Titchner
On This Earth
There is Something
to Live For, 2011.
Courtesy the artist and
Vilma Gold, London.

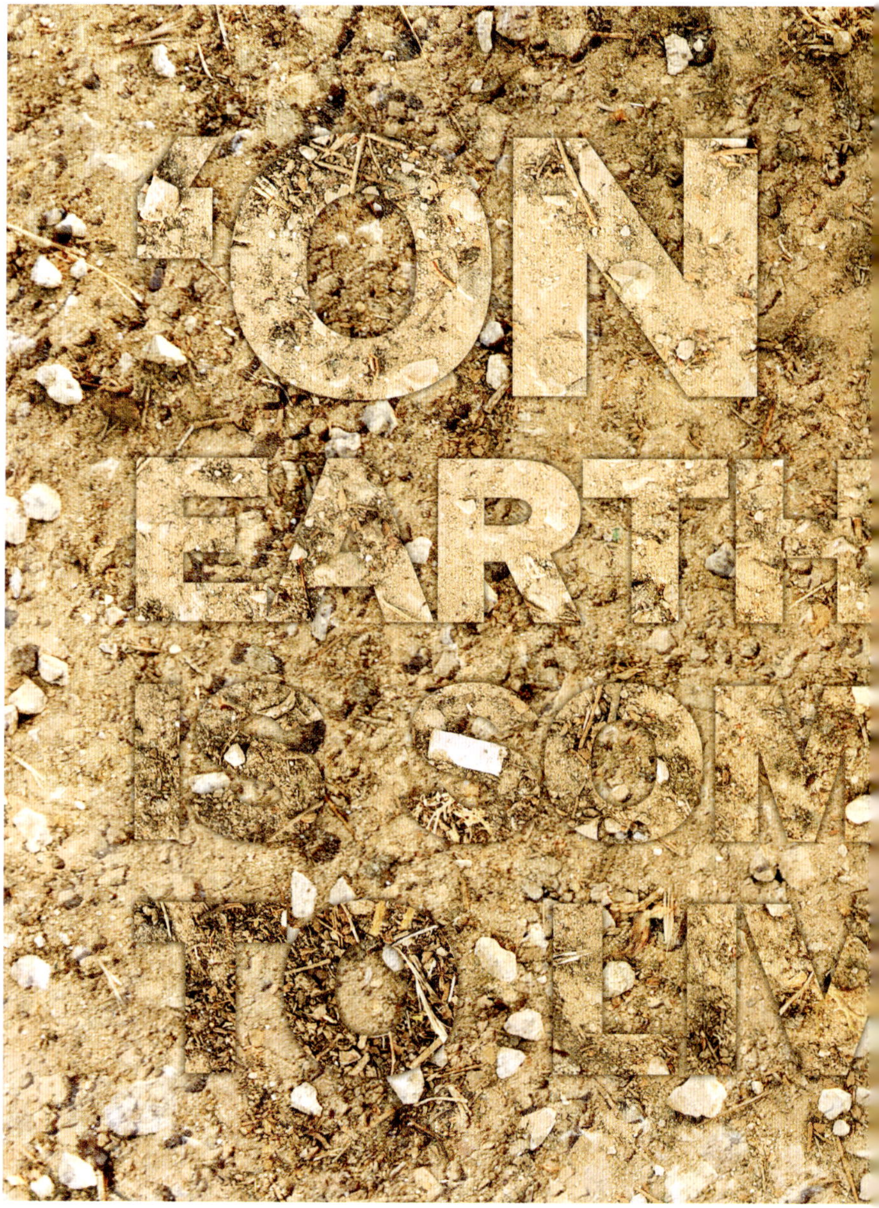

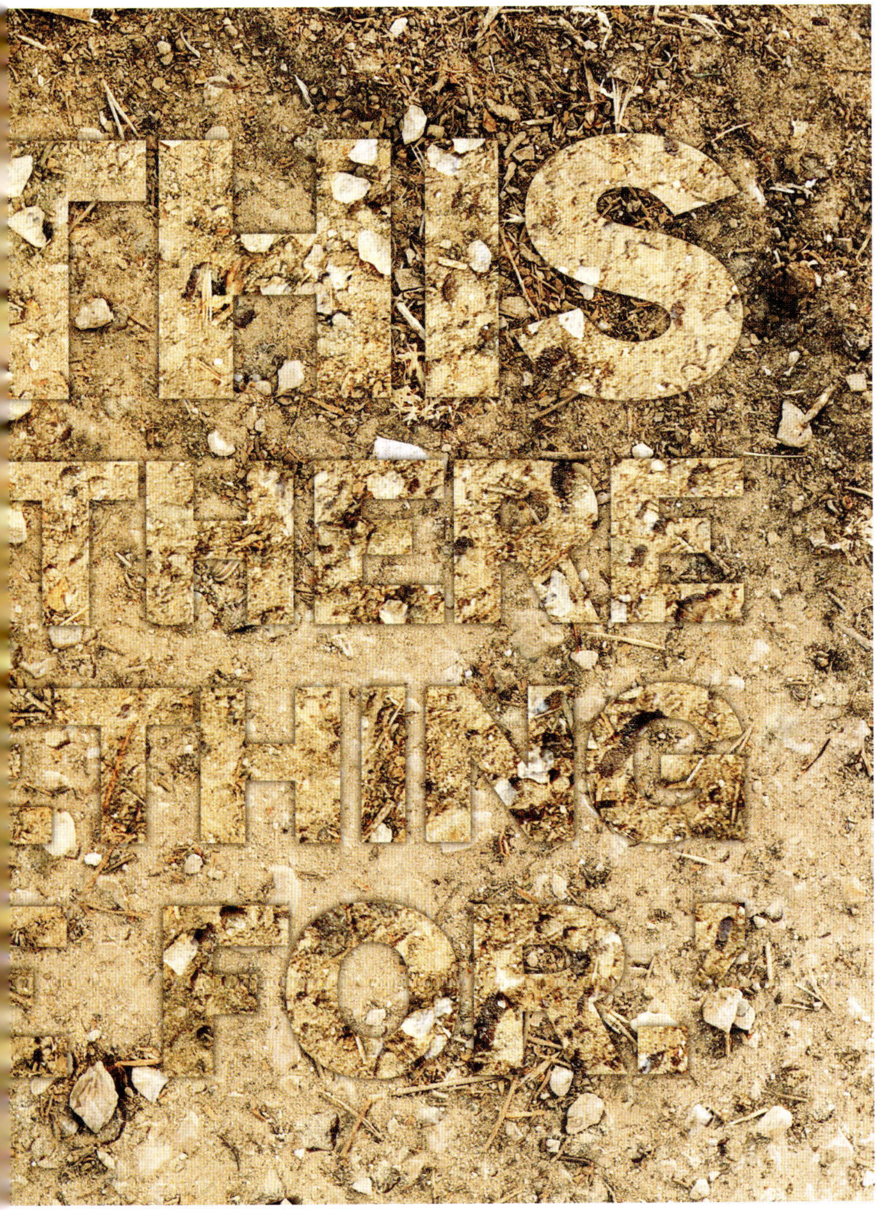
THIS
THERE
THING
FOR?

Mark Titchner
A Face Obscured, 2011.
Courtesy the artist and
Vilma Gold, London.

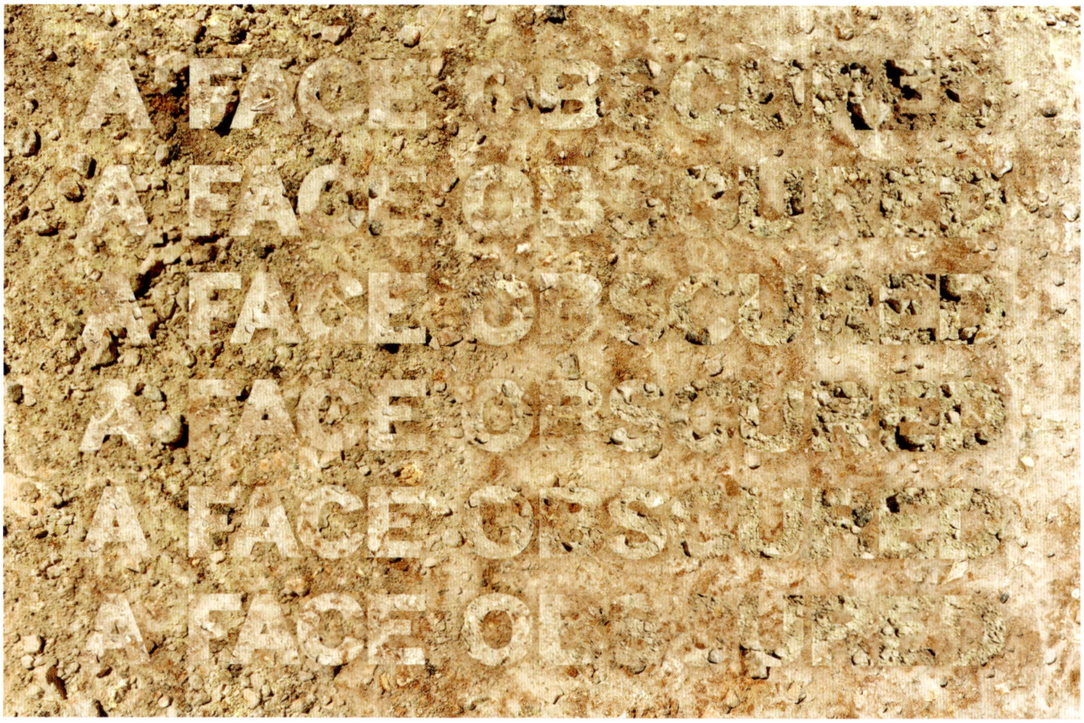

Mark Titchner
An Insistent Arm, 2011.
Courtesy the artist and
Vilma Gold, London.

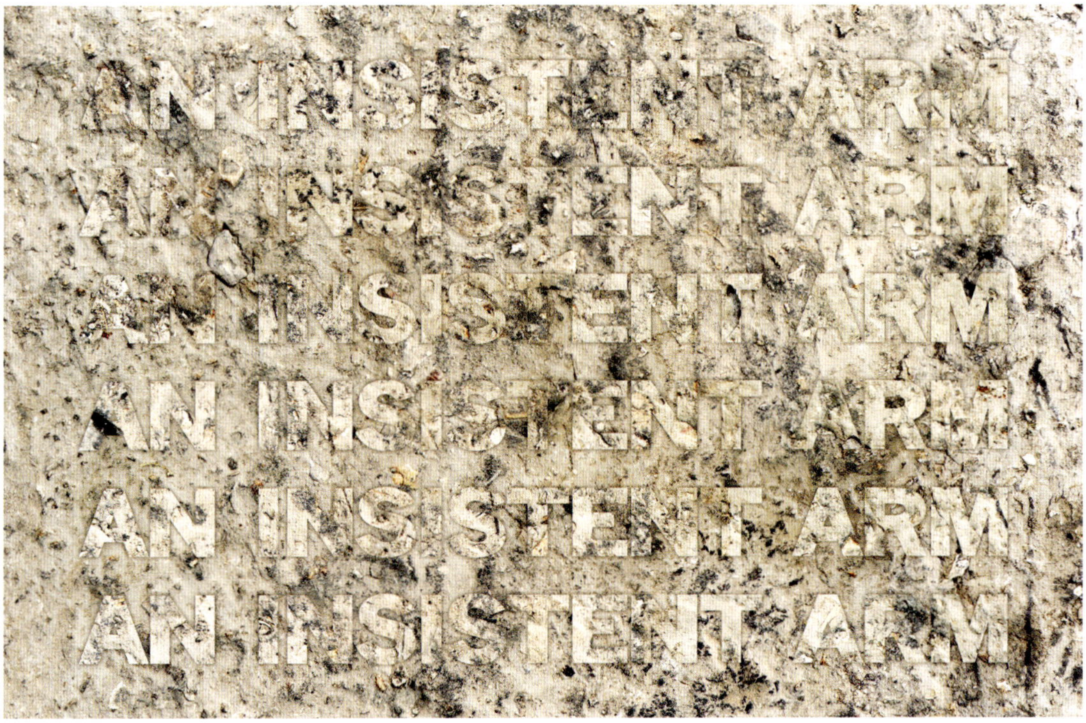

Mark Titchner
A Grimace Fixed, 2011.
Courtesy the artist and
Vilma Gold, London.

Mark Titchner
A Faltering Path, 2011.
Courtesy the artist and
Vilma Gold, London.

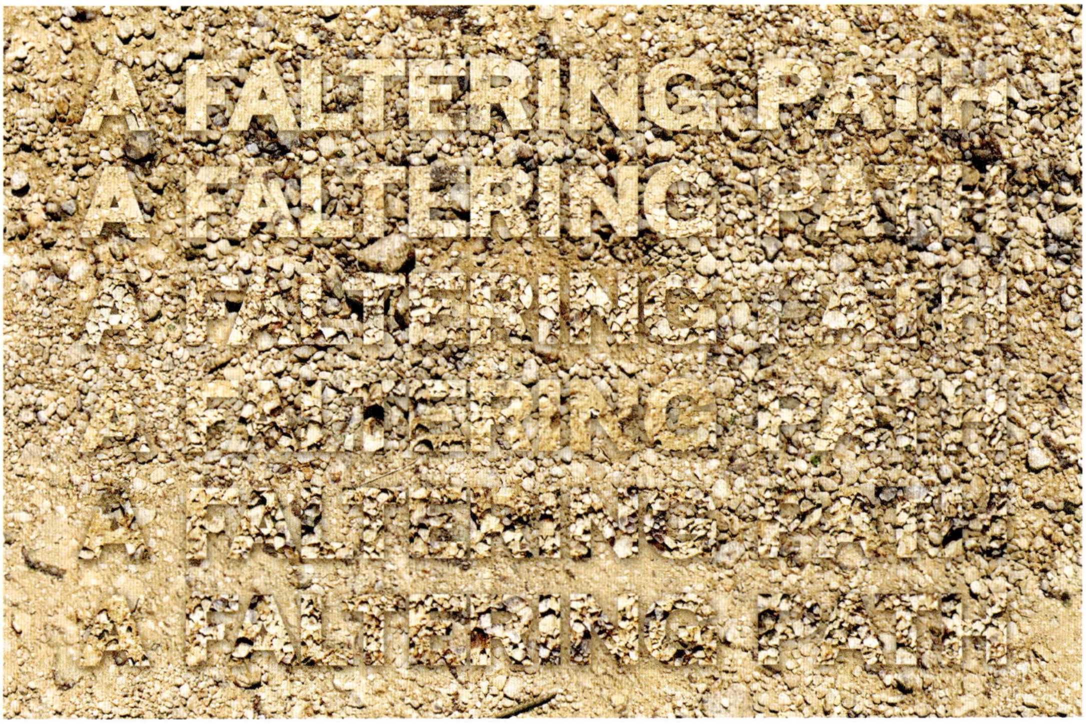

Sharif Waked
Beace Brocess #2
Plate #2, 2011.
From a series of
16 plates, Ink and
highlighter pen on
paper, 29.7 x 21 cm.
Courtesy the artist.

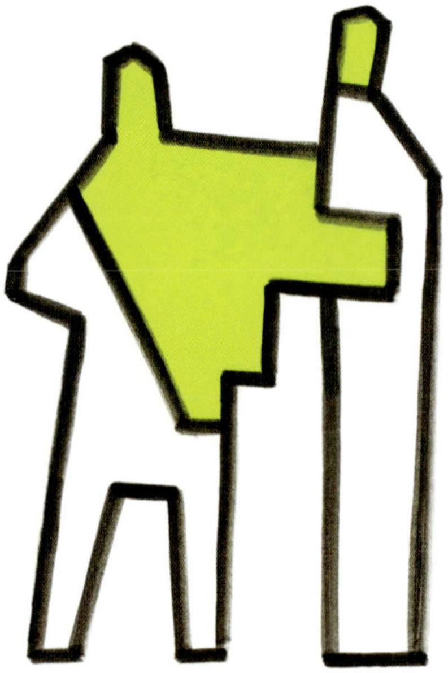

Beace Brocess #2
Plate #3, 2011.

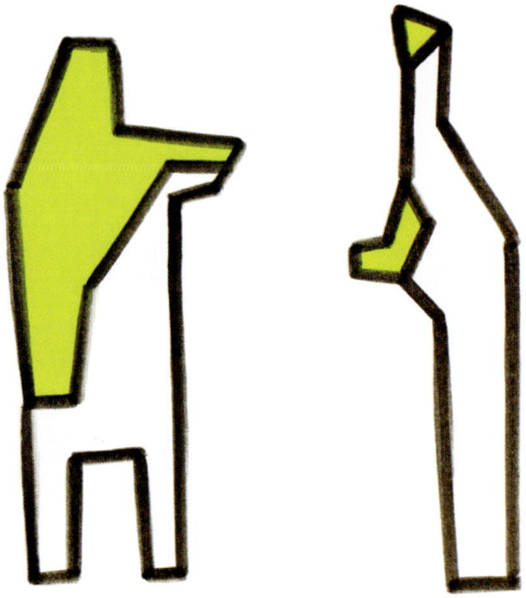

Beace Brocess #2
Plate #8, 2011.

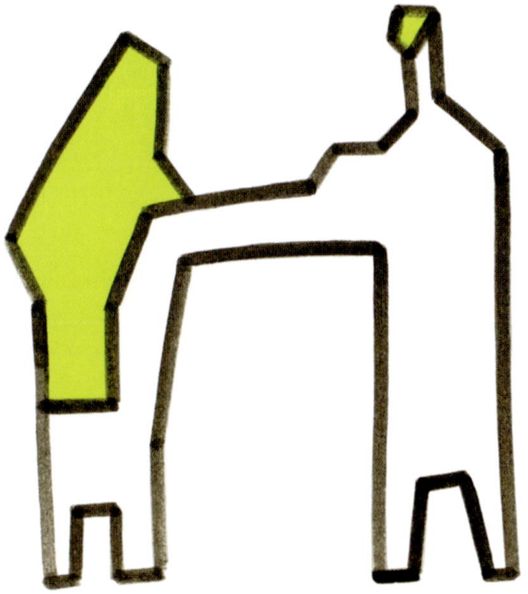

Beace Brocess #2
Plate #13, 2011.

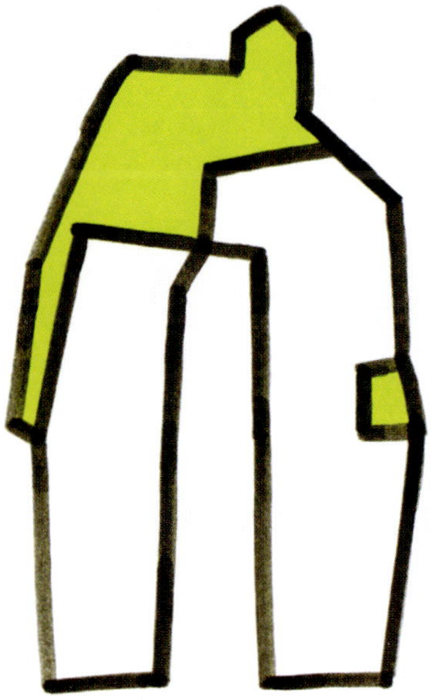

Beace Brocess #2
Plate #14, 2011.

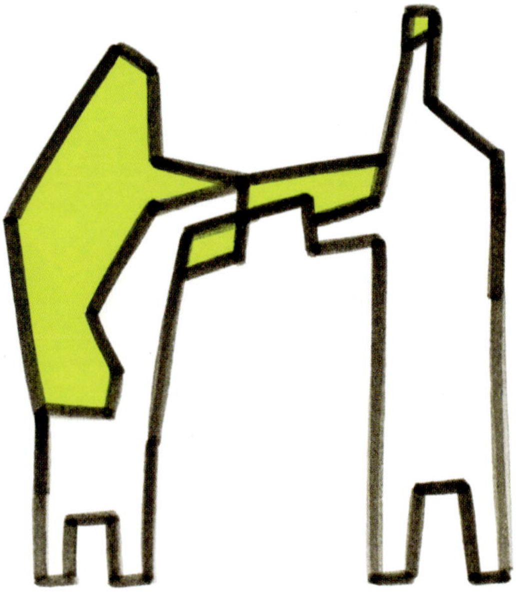

Beace Brocess #2
Plate #16, 2011.

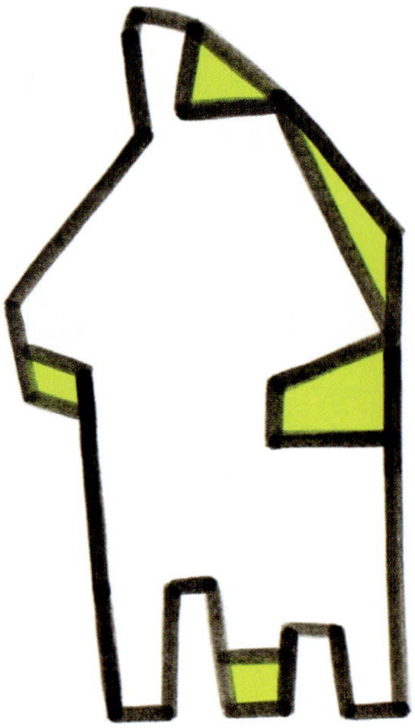

OPPOSITE &
FOLLOWING PAGES
Emily Jacir
Some things I probably should not say and some things I should have said
(fragments of a diary),
in "Palestine—Rien Ne Nous Manque Ici"
(ed. A Laidi-Hanieh, Cercle d'Art, Paris, 2008).

Some things I probably should not say and some things I should have said (fragments of a diary)

We are possibly the most discussed, yet most misrepresented people in the world. We are constantly dissected and examined by foreign 'experts' who 'explain' who we supposedly are. Additionally, an inordinate number of people have no problem claiming agency to speak on our behalf.

> June 1999
> I just moved to Ramallah and like half of this cities population I was not born here.
> I arrive to find all of us, all of us together. We are from Hebron, Jerusalem, Bethlehem, Gaza City, Jenin, Nablus and more. We are returnees with American accents. We are back from Kuwait, Saudi Arabia, and the UAE. We are from the dakhil with our Hebrew inflected Arabic. We came from Beirut and Tunis. We are the original residents of Ramallah. We are here from Jaffa, Lifta, and Lyd and came when we were expelled in 1948. We are in camps. We are in mansions. We are in middle class suburban homes. We are poor. We are rich.
> We are here. The city seems to be bursting with creative energy and hope.
> We are almost normal.
> Hope.
>
> September 2000.
> The intifada starts.
> Stop.
>
> Circle.

Ramallah became my home. For me it was our New York, full of artists, filmmakers, musicians, activists, and all kinds of returnees. I felt like we were a thousand fragments all coming together and building something new. It was there that I could find pieces from all our narratives. I had always abhorred the idea that the Palestinian narrative in the West Bank or Gaza was the main or the real narrative while our stories in Lebanon, Syria, Tunis, Riyadh, Paris and Rome were somehow "less" Palestinian or negated.

I want all our histories and narratives; every name, every village, every story, every account, every version, every attempt, every artifact, every battle, everything. All of it. No matter where it took place.

It is from Ramallah that I run circles with Adania and Rizek in London, Hasan in New York, Alia in Beirut, Salim in airports…and Annemarie always.

February 2008 Chicago
I am at Northwestern University teaching this semester and it is a cold snowy winter night with harsh winds blowing in from the lake. I am lost amongst the snowdrifts and the large heavy snowflakes amassing around me. My phone rings and breaks the silence.
Salim is calling me from a random airport in America. He is teaching at Berkeley this semester. He has just gotten off the phone with Issam, who is on his way here to give a lecture to my class. Issam arrives and tells me that Farid will be down at Southern Illinois next week.
Everything makes perfect sense. I know exactly where I am.

You also have the option of leaving in a way that many who are there don't have. How do you deal with the reality of that tension?
How can I explain to the journalist that the question is exactly backwards and that the option of staying is where the tension lies? That the tension I feel exists precisely when I am in Palestine because so many do not have the option of ever entering our country. Most of our people are forbidden from entering and have never had the privilege of setting one foot in their homeland. In each step I take is the painful awareness of all those who can not walk on this land, who are denied entry, who are forbidden from staying, from returning, or even from simply visiting.

Meanwhile the Arab journalist wants a hero or a martyr and will create one if necessary.

October 2007 Ramallah
I am out with Reem and Mai. A Scotsman asks us how long we have lived in Ramallah. He doesn't understand why we are here. I remark on the fact that I am only questioned like this about Ramallah. The fact that I was not born or raised in New York but decided to make it my home is something no one ever questions or challenges. Not so with Ramallah, we are constantly affronted for making this a home.

Allah

Why won't you translate it? There is simply no logical reason for this buffoonery. Why use an Arabic word in your news reports when there is an equivalent word in English (French, Italian, Spanish…) that means exactly the same thing?

The media's use of the word "Allah" rather then "God" is of course a deliberate move. This effect helps construct an "otherness" which keeps us distant and thus makes it easier to demonize and make it sound like pagan or barbaric God. It is also an effective way to sever it from its local context of having a historical and theological connection to Christianity and Judaism. If people knew that it was simply "God", the same as their God and that in reality Arabic speakers of ALL faiths (and that includes Christians and Jews) use the word Allah for God they might actually begin to understand something. By not translating "Allah", they are propagating the views of those who view the world as a "clash of civilizations". On the other hand there are those in our community who are only too happy to continue this false construction in an effort to appear more mysterious.

February 2006 Amman
Amman the city of lost souls.
What Palestinian doesn't have an aunt in Amman?
Ya Amman
Waiting room turned permanent.
Transit point for so many.
You keep accumulating Palestinians, Iraqis and others.
Oh Amman dumping ground of all our region's conflicts.
How many times 1948? 1967?
Palestinians from Kuwait…has it really been 15 years since we left?
And the cars go to Damascus, Beirut, Baghdad , the jisr
and we wait.
And the cars keep circling in the duwar never reaching their destination

Whisky in a late night bar
"Wayn a Ramallah" sings the musician
Raed jumps up onto the table and I follow
And Palestine is right over there…
And in the duwar the cars circle
Around and around and around
Never reaching their destination
Never finding their way home
Each duwar the final stop for those lost here.

"I am going crazy with what is going on. I can't sleep. My head is going to explode. Are you in Palestine or New York?"

But your name is Emily?
Yes, my name is Emily. I really do not understand why this is so surprising. I was named after my teta (grandmother). There were many women of her generation of various faiths who had the name Emily. I am very sorry that you think it is not Palestinian enough… perhaps not different enough. It may come as a shock to you but we are a very old culture and our land has been under numerous invaders, occupiers, visitors, tourists and guests and like all people on this earth we are not stagnant. We take in new names and they become part of us and part of our ever-growing and ever-changing culture.

After 9/11, all the shades of grey in the world seem to be slowly disappearing. All of a sudden names like Osama, Suleiman, Nasri, Nakhla, Fadi, Kareem are deemed "Muslim"names. Christians who carry those names are not counted. In America I find that some Arabs no longer know their own history and seem all to happy to define themselves according to the reductive definitions created by the media. Alternatively, in an effort to "preserve" our culture, some have become consumed with trying to remain rigid and fixed.

September 2005 Ramallah
My phone is ringing like crazy. Everyday there seems to be a new international group coming in to do an art project. I lie on my bed and stare at the ceiling. I don't want to answer the phone anymore. I don't want to meet any more foreigners. I am too exhausted. This feels like an onslaught of art missionaries. All of a sudden there seems to be a plethora of projects using Palestinians as subject matter. Palestinians are asked to dance, to sing, to spray paint, to recite texts, recount hardships…

April 1995 Dallas
I am at an opening of an exhibition at the Irving Arts Center in which I am presenting a series of large-scale paintings I made in 1994 inspired by photographs I had taken during the first Intifada. The photos were of the layers of graffiti, which had accumulated on the walls of Bethlehem. In my paintings I incorporated this use of layering and graffiti, and used languages from countries I had lived in like Italian, Arabic and English to speak.
All of a sudden I see an 85-year-old man standing with his cane in front of my work. He is really seeing my work and I can see that it is speaking to him in a way it isn't speaking to anyone else. I sense that he knows Palestine…

In that moment I understood everything and I saw exactly whom I was speaking to. I met him and learned that his name was Munir Bayoud – Allah yerhamu. He once taught at the Orthodox High School in Jaffa and later at St. George's College in Jerusalem.
Thank you Munir.

Thank you to the man in Wichita from Borj il Barajneh who took care of me and the Imam who told everyone in Friday prayers to come attend my exhibition. Thank you to the couple (also from Borj il Barajneh) that smiled at me and yelled "Salaam!" across the stiff exhibition hall in St. Gallen. There are too many to list but wherever I am grounded because of you. Thank you.

From: hasanhourani@hotmail.com
Subject: zaitouzaater performance
Date: July 20, 2001 5:39:17 PM EST
To: ejacir@usa.net

Dear friends,

Hasan Hourani will be performing in Union Square on Saturday August 4 from 3 until 9 p.m. Its a one day event, in which we will offer Palestinian food to passersby for free. Hasan will have a brochure to hand out which describes how we eat zait and zaater and a map of where it is found in Palestine. People will be invited to eat some zait and talk with us about this Palestinian dish. There will also be samples for people to take home with them to try. The performers will be 5 old Palestinian women wearing our national dress. They will feed the people. There will also be live music by Palestinian musicians.

We are asking for your help.

We need people to donate zait ou zaater (as much or as little as you can offer), and also if you know any women who would be willing to come out and do this. We are in the process of collecting the zaater now, so if you can donate please e-mail Hasan at : hasanhourani@hotmail.com.

Thanks,

Hasan and Emily

September 2003 Ramallah
A British curator sits with me in a café smiles and says: "Everyone here must just hate the Americans"…as if we are in cahoots. I bite my tongue and simply respond no and in fact there are many American activists here doing solidarity work with us. I am struck by his ability to remove himself from his own history and British involvement in the Middle East…especially here.

June 2005 London.
It is a dark June night in London and Adania and I are walking under the street lamps. Near or far to each other or to Ramallah, we both know that the spaces between us are filled with particles of dust.

But you have an American accent?
I smile. The European is horrified by my American accent. I am not authentic enough; they are suspicious because they can't place me. They are shaken and can't locate me in their comfortable categorizing of the world. I have begun to really love my American accent simply for its effect on certain Europeans, particularly on those touring our region or who specialize in our suffering. Dissatisfied with my explanations and upset with the fact that I have the same mobility as them they move quickly on. I am on equal footing and there is no room for them to "help" me.
My American accent has saved me from being "saved".

August 2003 Bethlehem
I am drinking tea with my cousin and we are reminiscing about the days we used to be able to get in a car and drive to Ramallah.
We sound like our grandmothers talking about going to Jaffa.

May 2001 New York City
Hasan, Zafer and I agree to meet in Union Square with our arghiles. We sit and smoke and watch the world whirling around us.

November 11 2004
Arafat has died. World leaders go to Cairo to pay their respects to our leader. I am consumed by this spectacle, which is taking place not on our land but in a foreign land, in the space of an airport, in a place of transit, a space of endless departure where you never arrive. Later Arafat is brought to Ramallah to his final resting place, which is actually temporary.

Where are you from?
This is the hardest question to answer because our answers never satisfy you, or are unacceptable in your eyes.
In fact, we know exactly where we come from and exactly where we belong but for some reason this seems incomprehensible to anyone else but ourselves. We are constantly questioned and doubted. In extreme cases we are simply told that that in fact is not where we are from.

Addendum to "Where We Come From":

I find it very telling that this work has been consistently misnamed and misunderstood. It is not "Where Do We Come From?" or "Where Are We Coming From" or the myriad of other variants that I have seen published. It is not a question nor is there the slightest hesitation.

Additionally, it was based on my "freedom of movement" as a Palestinian with an American passport, a document which allowed me this basic human right. I utilized my passport to access Palestine for Palestinians (BOTH inside and outside the country) who are prohibited entry into their own homeland and/or who are restricted movement within it. This is no longer the case and this piece would be impossible to make today. I can no longer move freely through the borders with my American passport. I am no longer allowed to enter Gaza, and certain Palestinian towns in the West Bank.

Since making the work in 2002, Israel has also implemented an undeclared policy of denying entry and/or re-entry to the occupied Palestinian territories on a much larger scale. Those who are denied entry and have the highest risk of deportation are Palestinians who hold foreign passports (American and EU passports especially), as well as children and/or foreigners who are married to someone with a Palestinian ID. Those that do have the ability to move are subjected to the worst forms of humiliation at every crossing in an effort to discourage people from entering or moving around the country. When will you understand that Israel has complete control over the population of the Occupied Palestinian Territories, and the only way to enter is via Israeli ports of entry? Israel decides who gets in and who does not by granting visas and permits to enter. Meanwhile the calculated fragmentation of our people and our lands into smaller and smaller spaces continues. Israel has implemented some of the most draconian and violent military tactics in history to prevent us from entry into our own homeland as well as the ability to move freely within it. These measures have been designed to fragment and destroy the fabric of our entire people. I am not sure how many different ways we are going to have to tell you this until you hear us.

September 2005 Rome
I go to Termini and pretend I am going somewhere.
I sit for hours to hear the announcements and to feel all the people swirling around me with their suitcases.

Biographies

Guy Mannes-Abbott is a writer, essayist and critic who lives and works in London. He is the author of a singular series of texts-poems, stories, aphorisms—called e.things which have been exhibited, published and performed alongside the work of leading British artists as well as sporing artist's videos, since 1997. In Ramallah, Running is the longest and latest in this series of texts and projects. Mannes-Abbott has recently collaborated with Bombay-based collective CAMP on a film called *The Country of the Blind, and Other Stories* for the Folkestone Triennial 2011, as well as, for example, written catalogue essays on visual art. He has been a tutor in architectural theory at the Architectural Association School of Architecture, London and published in specialist journals. Critical journalism spanning literature and visual art has appeared in the *New Statesman, The Guardian, Harpers & Queen, TANK, Bidoun* and *The Independent*. Recent publications include; *Translated By* (Ed. Arsène-Henry & Basar), and an Introduction to Mourid Barghouti's *Midnight and Other Poems*. A novel set between the Arabian and Baltic Seas is forthcoming.

Samar Martha is co-founder and director of "ArtSchool Palestine" and a freelance curator. Martha has worked with Visiting Arts—London on a range of projects across the Middle East. She is a co-founder of Al Mamal Foundation for Contemporary Art— Jerusalem. Martha has been writing, lecturing and curating exhibitions in the UK and abroad with a particular focus on Palestinian and Middle Eastern contemporary art practices, such as This Day at Tate Modern, 2007, Still on Vacation at Nobel Peace Centre, Oslo, 2007, solo exhibitions by artist Khalil Rabah 50,320 Names at Brunei Gallery, London, 2007, and In/Scene video art exhibition at Al Hoash Gallery—Jerusalem, 2008; Mapping an exhibition by Palestinian artists at Dubai, 2009, The Other Shadow of the City an international art exhibition at Al Hoash Gallery Jerusalem, 2009; In/Progress at Forum Schlossplatz, Aarau, Switzerland, 2010, Localities at the Rokensdile Museum, Denmark, 2010; and Future Movements Jerusalem at Liverpool Biennial, 2010. Since 2005 she has co-curated the annual Palestine Film Festival at the Barbican Centre, London.

Jananne al-Ani was born in Kirkuk, Iraq in 1966 and lives and works in London. She has had solo shows at Darat al Funun, Amman, 2010; Tate Britain, London, 2005; and the Freer Gallery of Art and Arthur M. Sackler Gallery, Washington DC, 1999. Selected group exhibitions include Topographies de la Guerre, Le Bal, Paris, 2011; The Future of a Promise, 54th Venice Biennale, 2011; Closer, Beirut Art Center, 2009; The Screen-Eye or the New Image: 100 Videos to Rethink the World, Casino Luxembourg, 2007; and Without Boundary: Seventeen Ways of Looking, Museum of Modern Art, New York, 2006. She has also co-curated exhibitions including Veil, 2003/2004 and Fair Play, 2001/2002. Al-Ani is recipient of the Abraaj Capital Art Prize, 2011, and the East International Award, 2001. Her work can be found in several collections among them the Tate Gallery, Arts Council and Imperial War Museum, London; the Pompidou Centre and Fondation Louis Vuitton pour la Création, Paris; the Smithsonian Institution, Washington DC; and Darat al Funun, Amman. Al-Ani's photographic work is represented by Rose Issa Projects, London.

Francis Alÿs was born in Antwerp, Belgium in 1959. He studied engineering and history of architecture before relocating to Mexico City in 1986 where he lives and works. From early on walks and urban strolls took a central role in his practice, as with *The Collector*, 1991–1992, and *Paradox of Praxis 1 (Sometimes Doing Something Leads to Nothing)*, 1997, where he pushed a block of ice until it melted completely. In 2002 Alÿs orchestrated *The Modern Procession* for the Museum of Modern Art (MoMA) in New York using 150 volunteers. In 2002 he also produced *When Faith Moves Mountains* with Rafael Ortega and Cuauhtémoc Medina, requiring 500 volunteers to move a 500 metre-long sand dune a few centimeters. Alÿs's exhibitions include 5th Havana Biennale, Cuba, 1994; Walks/Paseos, Museo de Arte Moderno, México DF, 1997; The Green Line, The Israel Museum, Jerusalem, 2005; Seven Walks, in collaboration with Artangel, London, 2005; 49th and 52nd Venice Biennales, 2001 and 2007, Italy; Fabiola, Dia Art Foundation, New York, LACMA, Los Angeles and National Portrait Gallery, London, 2007–2009; 8th Panama Biennale, Panama, 2008; 7th Gwangju Biennale, South Korea, 2008; A Story of Deception, Tate Modern, London, Wiels, Belgium, MoMA, New York, 2010–2011.

Najwan Darwish is a poet, critic and literary editor. He lives in Jerusalem, Palestine and contributes to Palestinian cultural life through several key projects and initiatives in Palestine and abroad. In 2009 Najwan was selected by the Beirut39 Festival as one of the best Arab-language writers under the age of 39. His poems have been translated into numerous languages and have appeared in a number of publications around the world. In addition, he has written widely on Palestinian art, and contributed to several contemporary art magazines and platforms, most recently Ibraaz.com (a publishing forum on the MENA region edited by critic Anthony Downey). He is the editor of the *Min wa Ila* magazine, which publishes the works of young Arab writers and artists in the region. Najwan's first poetry collection *He was Knocking at the Last Door* was published in 2000. His most recent book is "Je me lèverai un jour"; a selection of his poetry in French selected and translated by Antoine Jockey.

Jean Fisher first studied Zoology, later taking a degree in Fine Art. She subsequently became a freelance writer on contemporary art and colonial legacies, and has worked closely with artists and critics from Ireland, Native America, Cuba, Mexico and the Black British diaspora. During several years in NYC she co-curated exhibitions of contemporary Native American art with the artist Jimmie Durham. She is a former editor of *Third Text*, and editor of the anthologies *Global Visions: Towards A New Internationalism in the Arts*, 1994, *Re-verberations: Tactics of Resistance, Forms of Agency*, 2000, and with the Cuban critic and curator Gerardo Mosquera, *Over Here: International Perspectives on Art and Culture*, 2004. She lives in London, and is Visiting Professor in Contemporary Curating at the Royal College of Art, and Professor of Fine Art and Transcultural Studies at Middlesex University.

Emily Jacir's work spans a diverse range of media and strategies including film, photography, social interventions, installation, performance, video, writing and sound. Recurrent themes in her practice include repressed historical narratives, resistance, political land divisions, movement (both forced and voluntary) and the logic of the archive. Jacir has shown extensively throughout Europe, the Americas and the Middle East since 1994. Awards include a Golden Lion at the

52nd Venice Biennale, 2007, for her work *Material for a film*; a Prince Claus Award from the Prince Claus Fund in The Hague, 2007; and the Hugo Boss Prize at the Guggenheim Museum, 2008. In 2003, *Belongings* was published by OK Books, a monograph on a selection of Jacir's work from 1998–2003. Her second self-titled monograph was published by Verlag für moderne Kunst Nürnberg, in 2008. Full-time professor and on Academic Board of the International Academy of Art Palestine, 2006–2011. Resident Artist at the Home Workspace Program, Beirut 2011–2012.

Olaf Nicolai born in Halle ad Saale in 1962. He lives and works in Berlin. Nicolai has been awarded several grants and residencies, including the Studienstiftung des Deutschen Volkes at the Studies Centre for Art and Science in Venice, 1993; Villa Massimo, Rome, 1996; the PS 1 Museum Grant, New York, 1998; the IASPIS Grant, Stockholm, 2000; the Art Award Wolfsburg, 2002; and the Villa Aurora, Los Angeles, 2008. Since the early 1990s, his work has been displayed in many international group and solo exhibitions including documenta X, 1997; Venice Biennale, 2001 and 2005; Sydney Biennial, 2002; Gwangju Biennial, 2002; Sharjah Biennial, 2005; Athens Biennial, 2007, 3rd Riwaq Biennial, Ramallah, 2009, and the Biennial of Thesaloniki, 2011. His work is shown in institutions as Migros Museum, Zurich; Museo Serralves, Porto; Museum of Modern Art, New York; Fondation Cartier, Paris; Lenbachhaus, Munich among others. His sound installation with performances *Escalier du Chant* runs throughout this year at the Pinakothek der Moderne, Munich.

Paul Noble was born in 1963 in Dilston, Northumberland. He was one of five founding members of City Racing, an influential artists' space in London, 1988–1998, where he showed in 1990. His work has since been exhibited in London at Cubitt Gallery, 1995, Chisenhale Gallery, 1998, Tate Gallery, 1999, and Whitechapel Art Gallery, 2004; and internationally at the Albright Knox Gallery, Buffalo, 2003, Museum Boymans van Beuningen, Rotterdam and the Migros Museum, Zurich, 2005. Noble lives and works in London.

Khalil Rabah was born in Jerusalem and currently lives and works between London, New York and Ramallah. He has participated in a number of group exhibitions around the world, as well as several biennials, including the Sao Paulo, Sydney, Kwangju, Istanbul, Liverpool and Venice Biennales. Rabah has had numerous international solo shows and undertaken various artist-in-residency programs in Europe. His works include *United States of Palestine Airlines*, 2007, *50,320 Names*, 2007, *Biproduct*, 2010, and most recently *Art Exhibition, Ready-made Representations*, 2011, shown at Sharjah Biennial. Rabah has taught architecture at Birzeit University, Palestine and Fine Arts at Bezalel Academy, Jerusalem. He founded The Palestinian Museum of Natural History and Humankind, 2003–ongoing, and co-founded Al Ma'mal Foundation for Contemporary Art in Jerusalem and ArtSchool Palestine in London. He is the Director of the Riwaq Biennial, Palestine. Rabah also serves on the advisory boards of Delfina Foundation and the Biennial Foundation, and is a member of the Curricular Committee of Home Workspace Program (Ashkal Alwan, Beirut).

Adania Shibli born in Palestine in 1974, has twice been awarded the Young Writer's Award–Palestine by the AM Qattan Foundation, for her novels *Touching*, al-Adab, 2002, and *We are All Equally Far from Love*, al-Adab, 2004. Her short stories and essays have been translated into French, German, Italian, Hebrew, Korean, and English. English translations of her work have appeared or are forthcoming in the Iowa Review, Words Without Borders, and Banipal. Her play *The Error* has been staged at the Tristan Bates Theatre, London, and as part of the New Works festival at the New World Theater in Amherst, Massachusetts. Shibli has a PhD in media and cultural studies from the University of East London. She is currently living in Berlin where she has a postdoctoral fellowship.

Mark Titchner was born in Luton in 1973, studied at Central Saint Martins and now lives and works in London. He works in a wide range of media including sculpture, installations, banners, posters, video and performance. He frequently explores the ways in which communication engenders belief and the ways in which our minds can be subtly manipulated. Text commonly features within his work and he draws from a wide range of sources including song lyrics, advertising, utopian statements and political manifestos. He recently exhibited Be True To Your Oblivion a solo show at the New Art Gallery, Walsall and was included in Nothing is Forever at South London Gallery and The Dark Monarch at Tate St Ives, 2010. Titchner was nominated for the Turner Prize in 2006 and has had solo museum shows at the Hellenic American Union, 2009, BALTIC, Gateshead, 2008 and 2007, and Arnolfini, 2006. In 2012 he will have a solo show at the Macedonian Museum of Contemporary Art, Thessaloniki, Greece. He is represented by Vilma Gold, London.

Sharif Waked was born in Nazareth to a Palestinian refugee family from the village of Mjedil. He lives and works in Haifa/Nazareth. Waked has exhibited at various biennials, museums, and art venues internationally including: 2011: Barjeel Art Foundation, Sharjah, UAE; 2010: Royal Academy of Arts, Piccadilly, London; Diverse Works, Houston, Texas. 2009: Museum of Modern Art of Algiers; Spaport Biennial, Banja Luka, Bosnia-Herzegovina; The Institut du Monde Arabe, Paris; Queens Museum of Art, NY; 2008: Bluecoat Gallery, Liverpool; Haifa Museum of Art; Artists Space, New York; Stephen Lawrence Gallery, London; The Seconde Riwaq Biennale, Ramallah; Tate Modern, London; The Imperial Mint, Topkapi Palace, Istanbul; Witte de Witt Museum, Rotterdam; Home Works II, Beirut; Khalil Sakakini Cultural Centre, Ramallah. Waked's work is part of the permanent collections of the Solomon R Guggenheim Museum; Sharjah Art Foundation; Fondation Louis Vuitton pour la création; Israel Museum; Queensland Art Gallery; and the Barjeel Art Foundation among others.

Acknowledgements

Guy Mannes-Abbott and Samar Martha would like to thank all the artists and writers who have responded with such generosity and commitment to this project.

ArtSchool Palestine would like to thank the Sharjah Art Foundation for their generous support in making this project possible. Special thanks goes to Charles Asprey, Zina Jardaneh, Sawsan Asfari and Rana Sadik for their support in realising this project.

Guy Mannes-Abbott and Samar Martha would also like to thank the following;

Hazem Alnamla
Mourid Barghouti
Husam and Amal Barghouti
Sacha Craddock
Mahmoud Abu Hashhash
Iyad Issa
Yazan Khalili
AM Qattan Foundation
Sahar Qawasmi
Dr Joerg Schumacher
Azmi Shunnarah
Ahdaf Soueif
Sanna Wennberg
Raouf Haj Yahya

SHARJAH ART FOUNDATION

ArtSchool Palestine
منتدى الفنون المعاصرة

Colophon

Black Dog Publishing Limited
10a Acton Street, London
WC1X 9NG
United Kingdom

Tel: +44 (0)20 7713 5097
Fax: +44 (0)20 7713 8682
info@blackdogonline.com
www.blackdogonline.com

British Library Cataloguing-in-Publication Data.
A CIP record for this book is available from the British Library.

ISBN 978 1 907317 67 5

Black Dog Publishing Limited, London, UK, is an environmentally responsible company. *In Ramallah, Running* is printed on FSC certified paper.

reuse recycle reduce

architecture art design
fashion history photography
theory and things

black dog publishing
london uk

www.blackdogonline.com